ILLUSTRATIONS

xi

ILLUSTRATIONS

x ILLUSTRATIONS

CONTENTS

WAR FOR THE WORLD

A CHRONICLE OF
OUR FIGHTING FORCES
IN WORLD WAR II
BY FLETCHER PRATT

NEW HAVEN: YALE UNIVERSITY PRESS
TORONTO: GLASGOW, BROOK & CO.
LONDON: GEOFFREY CUMBERLEGE
OXFORD UNIVERSITY PRESS
1950

Copyright, 1950, by Yale University Press

WAR FOR THE WORLD

.·.

CHAPTER I

THE JAPANESE ATTACK

At 7:55 on the morning of December 7, 1941, the full air groups from six Japanese carriers appeared simultaneously over Pearl Harbor and the various air bases on Oahu Island in the Hawaiian Islands. At 7:58 the bombs began to drop and the commander of the naval air station shouted into a radio transmitter powerful enough to carry far across the Pacific: "Air raid on Pearl Harbor! This is no drill!"

At that moment, while two Japanese "peace envoys" were handing to Secretary of State Cordell Hull a note which caused that usually reserved old gentleman to turn white with rage, the United States had eight of its fifteen first-line battleships at anchor in the harbor, just preparing for the morning raising of the colors and the ceremonies incident upon beginning a day of rest. Seven cruisers were with them, and three destroyers were

in dry dock. Many of the crews were ashore, the officers at the Royal Hawaiian presumably sleeping off the effects of the previous night's festivities, the enlisted men in somewhat less pretentious establishments.

Of the remaining battleships one was near Puget Sound, while the other six were in the Atlantic, where German submarines had been making an active but undeclared war on us and had already torpedoed three United States warships. Four of the seven aircraft carriers were also in the Atlantic; so were several of the 37 cruisers and a large number of destroyers. Two of the other carriers were far to the west of Hawaii under cruiser escort, one of them having just delivered some Marine planes to the outpost at Wake Island; one carrier was at San Diego.

In the Philippines we had one heavy cruiser, an old and a new light cruiser, 12 old destroyers and 29 submarines, beside 30 patrol planes. All had been alerted for some time and were in a good state of readiness for war but short of crews. The supporting industrial machine had been set in motion by the war in Europe and a fleet outnumbering all the ships afloat was on the ways, but beyond two new battleships already running their shakedown cruises, nothing larger than a destroyer would join the battle line for a year to come.

The army was mostly scattered through training

camps in the Southern states. Following the Draft Act of 1940, it had been rapidly expanded from its pre-war strength of approximately 200,000 men to some 72 divisions, but the process involved the distribution of experienced soldiers throughout the mass, and fusion was still far from complete, as autumn maneuvers in Louisiana and the Carolinas had demonstrated. The production machinery of the nation had been thrown into high gear, but the military articles produced had mainly gone to Britain, and there were grave shortages in tanks, heavy artillery, planes, and even rifles. American troops were in Iceland and construction work was in progress on a chain of sea and air bases from that point along the Atlantic to Trinidad, title to land having been acquired by lease from England in exchange for fifty old destroyers. None of these bases was as yet complete.

THE Japanese attack on Pearl Harbor was planned with great care and was extraordinarily successful, being much aided by two factors. One was the neat American method of lining up planes wing to wing across an airfield. The earliest waves of attack fell on these parked planes and the run-ways from which they might have operated. When Rear-Admiral Bellinger of the Naval Air Force tried to get planes off at the height of the attack, he found only three out of 202 capable of flight.

The army record was approximately the same, nearly all of its 273 planes being wrecked in this first rush.

The second factor was careful Japanese scouting, partly no doubt by spies, but more immediately by midget submarines with two-man crews, one of which was sunk at the entrance to the harbor by the destroyer *Ward* just before the attack came in. At least two other midgets got into the harbor and made a complete tour of it. The information they transmitted was not altogether accurate but it was sufficient for the Japanese dive bombers and torpedo planes that followed the first wave to come in without hesitation on the battleships as they lay moored in a long double row beside Ford Island at the center of the harbor. The enemy planes were armed with heavy armor-piercing shells to which wings had been affixed for bombing purposes and with a specially designed torpedo of very short run and high explosive power.

The battleship *Arizona* got one of the bombs either through a turret or down her stack. It reached the forward magazines and she blew up. The battleship *Oklahoma* capsized as the result of several torpedo hits; *West Virginia* received no fewer than six torpedoes and settled to the bottom with her decks awash; *California* similarly settled, her fuel tanks ruptured and the ship ringed with fire; *Pennsylvania* had a bad bomb hit forward and was

further damaged when two destroyers in the dock with her went up in flames and exploded; *Maryland* had two heavy bomb hits and settled by the head. Of the remaining battleships, *Tennessee*, not much damaged, was wedged against a dock by the sunken *West Virginia*. *Nevada* got underway to stand out at the harbor, but this made her a target for every Japanese plane in the vicinity and she was so badly hit that she had to be beached in the entrance. Three of the light cruisers were seriously damaged, another destroyer had her bows blown off, and the mine layer *Oglala* was sunk. So was the target-ship *Utah*, which had erroneously been reported as a carrier by the Japanese scouts and so received one of the heaviest attacks of all.

The immediate price of their treacherous victory to the Japanese was fifty-odd planes shot down during the action, about half by army pursuit ships that succeeded in taking the air. On the American side, the American Pacific Fleet had practically ceased to exist, and a new command setup had to be made on the spur of the moment, since neither the public nor their own officers would have any confidence in the leaders who had been so taken by surprise—Admiral Husband E. Kimmel of the Pacific Fleet and Lieutenant-General Walter Short of the Hawaiian Command. It was obvious that the Philippines could not be held. There was nothing in existence that could interfere with a Japanese

intention to put in as many as fifty divisions, if necessary, against the two-division strength that held the islands. The Pacific question, in a military sense, was purely one of whether the Japanese could be restrained from the conquest of Australia. Meanwhile the President was preparing a declaration of war which was voted on the morning of December 8, over the odd objection of a single member that the news from Pearl Harbor might not be true. It was also obvious that the Germans and Italians would come into the war against us, and that we should have their submarines in numbers off the Atlantic coast; possibly their airplanes over our cities.

There was a conference at the White House on the afternoon of the 7th and another at the Navy Department immediately. President Roosevelt brought in Admiral Ernest J. King from the Atlantic Fleet in the dual capacity of commander of forces afloat and Chief of Naval Operations. To Honolulu he sent Admiral Chester W. Nimitz, head of the Bureau of Navigation (Personnel), who was something of a specialist in personnel relations and could be counted upon to pull up the badly shattered morale of the fleet.

The carriers at sea were ordered toward the Japanese-held Marshalls, in which direction it was supposed that the enemy had gone. *Yorktown* and *Hornet*, carriers, were ordered from the Atlantic

and *Saratoga* from San Diego to make near Pearl Harbor a concentration that would have to bear the weight of the war till the battleships could be repaired. A number of big bombers originally destined for England were dispatched to Honolulu and so were all the navy patrol planes from the Pacific coast. An emergency appeal for shipyard workers to repair the damaged vessels was sent out (they had three of them at sea before Christmas); the army stepped up both its draft and its industrial programs; and by December 11, when Hitler's Germany followed Japan into war with the United States, there were already troopships on the tide bound westward.

RADIO TOKYO, which was later to develop so high an index of inaccuracy, announced on the morning after the attack of December 7, 1941, that five of our battleships had been destroyed and three of the carriers damaged beyond repair. From subsequent events it is evident this did not represent propaganda so much as a genuine Japanese appraisal of the result they had secured. They captured Guam on the third day of the war from a garrison less than 600 strong. Wake Island with the aid of the Marine planes held out until December 22 and acquired a considerable symbolic importance, but after it fell there was no longer any American post within the width of the Atlantic

from Japan, and the enemy felt secure against any counterattack for a long time to come.

His primary objective was the capture and exploitation of the supply storehouse of the East Indies, and he now turned in that direction without fear of interruption, since his attacks on American installations had succeeded in so immobilizing our forces that no counterattack was possible. French Indo-China had been seized earlier in the year, and a large portion of the Japanese fleet was based there. Simultaneously with the attack on Pearl Harbor Japanese planes struck at the British base at Singapore, though in smaller numbers and doing less damage, and a Japanese landing force was thrown on the northern shore of Malaya at Khota Baru. At the same time there were Japanese scout planes all around and over Luzon, and Davao in the southern Philippines was heavily attacked. But something went wrong with the timing, and the enemy made no effort against the stronger installations around Manila until nine hours after word of Pearl Harbor had reached both Admiral Thomas C. Hart of the Asiatic Fleet and General Douglas MacArthur of the Army in the Philippines.

The warning did not do much good. When the planes came in at noon on December 8 (10 hours after the attack on Pearl Harbor, but a day later by International time) they found that the army planes had flown one futile search mission and had

lined themselves up on Clark and Nichols Field.
Later, it was protested that dispersal areas were
lacking, but the responsibility both for this and
for the neat alignment rests rather clearly on General Douglas MacArthur as Area Commander.
Secretary of War Stimson had written in a report
not published till the turn of the year that the
army intended to place "radical reliance" on the
air arm for the defense of the islands. The pilots
were our best, the planes new, and very good. Two-
thirds of the fighters and more than half of the
bombers were destroyed in that first smash; and
after the Japanese forced a landing and got an air
strip established at Aparri at the northern tip of
the island, they rapidly wore the rest of our aviation out by mere continuous action.

To complete the disasters of the day, a heavy
force of Japanese bombers and torpedo planes
caught the British battleships *Repulse* and *Prince
of Wales* off the coast of Malaya without air cover
and sent them to the bottom, the only heavy ships
the Allies had in the East. The next day Japanese
bombers either from Indo-China or carriers out at
sea swept in deliberate procession across the navy
yard at Cavite. There were no fighters to disturb
them, and keeping above the fire of the old-model
short-range anti-aircraft guns, they patiently reduced the place to rubble, sinking an American
submarine during the process. In the initial moves

of the campaign the Japanese had driven our air force from the skies and our navy from the seas around the Philippines, at almost no cost to themselves. Now they came storming ashore at Vigan on the northwest coast of Luzon and along the southern peninsula of Legaspi to close in on Manila and trap MacArthur there.

The Lingayen Gulf landing (Vigan) was the heaviest, about 80,000 strong; this alone was far more than MacArthur's whole force. The invaders had so complete a control of the air that counter-attacks had to be local and delivered only by night, but the American lines held fairly firm till December 24, when still another Japanese force was put ashore on Batangas Peninsula, south and west of the capital. A Japanese break-through on any of the thinly held fronts would now expose the forces on all the others to being taken in the rear. Mac-Arthur declared Manila an open city. In accordance with a plan drawn several years before by a young staff officer called Major Dwight Eisenhower, MacArthur held hard in the fertile valley that runs from Lingayen to Manila, while drawing his forces from the other fronts to form a concentration on Bataan Peninsula.

The operation was beautifully executed and was complete by January 1, but meanwhile the Japanese savagely bombed Manila on several occasions, showing a preference for Sundays when they would

catch the maximum number of people in churches and arouse the greatest terror. They continued to put men ashore on Luzon till there were not far short of 250,000, but their difficulty was in using this large force effectively. Bataan is occupied by the Mariveles Mountains, which run so steeply to the sea along their western slope that it is often necessary to wade into the water to progress from north to south, while on the eastern, valleyward flank there is only a narrow cultivated zone between the mountains and the extensive swamps which covered MacArthur's right. The cultivated zone is mainly in rice and sugar, boggy ground which canalized the Japanese tanks along road lines and brought them under the fire of American artillery. The heavily wooded character of the mountains did not permit the enemy to make full use of his air force, and the familiarity of the Filipinos on our side with every inch of the ground prevented attempts at infiltration.

Two massive assaults, one on the west coast and one in the eastern zone, were broken up with heavy casualties. General Homma of the Japanese forces then brought up fresh troops and settled down to a hammering campaign, designed to wear out the defenders. MacArthur began to get into difficulties about food, ammunition, and medical supplies.

Early in February the War Department ordered him out of the Philippines and down to Australia

to take charge of the Allied Southwest Pacific Command. He escaped in a motor torpedo-boat, commanded by Lieutenant John D. Bulkeley, crawling by night among islands which were for the most part already in Japanese hands, and leaving the defense of Bataan in the hands of Lieutenant-General Jonathan Wainwright. The latter held out under daily attacks until April 8, his troops hoping against hope for relief, but on that day the accumulated shortages made it impossible to carry on. The peninsula was surrendered and a handful of American troops retired to the rock and tunnel fortress of Corregidor at the entrance of Manila Bay. The place stood through more than 260 air raids, but when the Japanese mounted heavy artillery on Mariveles Mountain and began to shell it at the end of April, the finish was in sight.

General Wainwright surrendered on May 6. Some 40,000 prisoners were taken there and on Bataan. They were treated with great barbarity; more than half of them died as the result of a long march under a hot sun without food or water or as the result of subsequent tortures in prison camps. They were the only fighting force in all the Indies that had paid for itself by the number of casualties it had inflicted.

CORREGIDOR flew the last American flag in the East. When the Japanese bombers made Manila Bay

untenable the American naval forces ran down to
Surabaya and fell under a joint command called
ABDA-flot (American-British-Dutch-Australian),
headed by Admiral Conrad Helfrich of the Dutch
Marine. He had two light cruisers, a flotilla leader
and six destroyers of his own, besides a number of
British ships, which, as they were mainly concerned
with the support of Singapore to the west, took
little part in the campaign; and a number of Dutch
submarines which aided the Americans in destruc-
tively raiding Japanese sea traffic and were the
most effective vessels of the combined squadron.

The ABDA-flot organization was set up on January 1, 1942; on the 11th the Japanese came down
with paratroops and landing forces at Tarakan in
Borneo and Menado at the tip of spidery Celebes
Island, taking both places easily and setting up air
strips to cover further advances.

They were impeded, but not very much, by the
operations of a handful of Dutch bombers and of
Patrol Wing 10, a formation composed of American
flying boats, which were such easy meat for the
swarms of Japanese fighters that they were known
as the "cold turkey squadron"; Macassar Strait,
where they principally operated, was known as
"turkey alley." Helfrich and those surrounding
him, fully realizing this was an air campaign,
cabled frantically for more planes, but the planes
were simply not in existence to send. On January

20 one of our submarines reported that a huge Japanese convoy was in Macassar Strait, obviously bound for Balikpapan, the biggest oil port of the region. Helfrich had the bulk of his little fleet out to the west covering convoys to Singapore, but he determined to try a night raid on this Japanese convoy and to rush the American light cruisers *Marblehead* and *Boise* up with four destroyers to make the raid on the night of the 23rd.

The operation began with misfortune. The *Boise* struck on an uncharted reef, ripped out part of her bottom, and was eliminated from the campaign. *Marblehead* had engine trouble, so the destroyers had to go in alone under Commander F. R. Talbot. At this time the Japanese were unable to operate their air scouts by night and Talbot kept his ships screened under the edge of the land during the day. He got right into the convoy as it lay off Balikpapan and four times marched back and forth among the crowded ships, firing torpedoes in both directions till the whole sea was ablaze. He escaped without losing a man, the first Allied victory of the war.

It did not halt the Japanese. By the beginning of February they had cleared all Malaya but Singapore Island itself, were in full possession of Balikpapan, and were so close to Amboina and Timor on the east that these places had to be abandoned without a fight. There was very little that could

be done in the direction of Singapore, but Helfrich thought he might delay the Japanese advance at the center long enough to enable some air strength to reach him. He organized a striking force consisting of his own two cruisers, two American cruisers and eight destroyers, for a heavy raid up Macassar Strait against a Japanese convoy that was gathering at Balikpapan under escort of three cruisers and ten destroyers.

Under the flag of Rear-Admiral Karel Doorman of the Dutch navy the Allied force steamed out of Surabaya on February 3. Next morning it was caught near Bali by nearly 50 Japanese bombers. There was no air cover and the anti-aircraft artillery of the ships was primitive. Both *Houston* and *Marblehead* were badly hit, the former losing her after turret, the latter so damaged that she was barely kept afloat till she could reach Tjilitjap on the southern coast of Java for temporary repairs and then take the long route around the Cape of Good Hope for home. The Japanese got their convoy through to seize Macassar on Celebes Island, and on February 19 were ashore on Bali. Singapore had fallen four days before; Japanese planes were all over Java and the seas south of it, but a shipment of American fighter planes was reported on the way and Helfrich tried once more.

This time it was a daring night raid on the Japanese ships in harbor east of Java, made by succes-

sive waves of American destroyers following the Dutch cruisers through the strait. The raid was a success, the enemy losing a number of vessels; but it did not drive him from Bali. Before the end of the month the Japanese were massing heavy forces at Bandjermasin north of the Java Sea for a landing on Java itself. On the 26th their invasion convoy put out from that port under heavy escort and Doorman sailed to meet them. Some of the British ships had fallen under his flag, but his losses had been severe as the result of Japanese bombing raids and all he could muster were two heavy cruisers, one the still-damaged *Houston*, three light cruisers, and ten destroyers.

They made contact with an enemy battle line of considerably greater force near Bawean Island on the afternoon of the 27th, and for a time there was a gunnery action in which the Allied ships had by no means the worst of it, driving two cruisers from the enemy line with severe damage. But then the British heavy cruiser *Exeter* was hit in the engine room, dropped out, and Doorman's squadron was thrown into confusion. Japanese planes kept dogging them in the twilight, Japanese ships appearing and disappearing along the horizon. Our side had lost two of its destroyers in the action; as it fell dark one and then the other of the Dutch cruisers suddenly blew up, apparently torpedoed by submarines. The remaining vessels scattered.

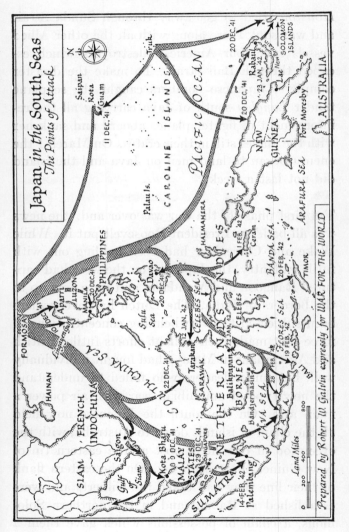

Japan in the South Seas
The Points of Attack

N

SAIPAN
Rota
Siam
Guam
11 DEC. '41

20 DEC. '41

TRUK

SOLOMON
ISLANDS

CAROLINE ISLANDS

PACIFIC OCEAN

Rabaul 23 JAN. '42
20 DEC. '41
Lae NEW

NEW GUINEA

Port Moresby

AUSTRALIA

Palau Is.

HALMAHERA

NETHERLANDS INDIES

1 FEB. '42
Ceram

BANDA SEA

20 FEB. '42

TIMOR

ARAFURA SEA

FORMOSA

Aparri 20 DEC. '41
LUZON
MANILA 20 DEC. '41

PHILIPPINES

Davao 20 DEC. '41

Sulu Sea

CELEBES SEA

12 JAN. '42

Tarakan
24 DEC. '41
SARAWAK

CELEBES

27 JAN. '42

FLORES SEA

19 FEB. '42

24 FEB. '42

BALI

HAINAN

SOUTH CHINA SEA

22 DEC. '41

BORNEO
Balikpapan
Bandjermasin

JAVA SEA

28

JAVA

FRENCH INDO-CHINA

Saigon
SIAM
Gulf of Siam

Kota Bharu 10 DEC. '41
29 DEC. '41
MALAY STATES
SINGAPORE

NETHERLANDS INDIES

SUMATRA
14 FEB. '42
Palembang

Land Miles
0 200 400 800

Prepared by Robert W. Galvin expressly for WAR FOR THE WORLD

Houston tried to get away through Sunda Strait and was sunk there along with all the other Allied vessels save four American destroyers which escaped through Bali Strait. To make the disaster complete, Japanese bombers caught the seaplane tender *Langley* south of Java carrying all the reinforcement of fighter planes aboard and sank her with the planes still in their crates. On March 1 the enemy began to land men on Java and the island did not last a week.

THE first phase of the war was over and "the news was all bad," as President Roosevelt put it. While Wake and Corregidor had been holding out with futile gallantry, the Japanese on the west had captured Rangoon and Mandalay and were now up to the borders of India. The Dutch had everywhere been subjected to overwhelming concentrations of force that made their gallant efforts futile; British and Australians in Malaya had fought individually well, but under leaders who failed to understand the new type of amphibian war with air power a main arm. On the south the Japanese now held all the chain of islands down to Australia, with the exception of one small post at the eastern tip of New Guinea, Port Moresby. On the eastern flank of their line they had taken the Gilberts and were established at Rabaul and in the northern Solomons, a chain of possessions which gave them a

vast triangular empire of sea and islands with its peak in the Kuriles. This empire was established by the middle of April, 1942. It contained all the supplies necessary to maintain war for the hundred years Japanese leaders foresaw it might last, and vast supplies of labor to exploit those resources.

The strategic sinew of that empire was the airplane. The first care of the invaders at every island was to set up air strips. They believed that when any point in their complex of islands was attacked the local defenses could instantly be supplemented from all the other bases within flight range, with a constant stream of planes being staged down from the homeland in the rear and still others hurried up by the forces afloat. They had demonstrated that planes could sink the heaviest ships in existence and that light ships were no match for an air attack. The outer chain of islands thus should be impenetrable in any practical sense, and behind that screen they could develop at their leisure the forces necessary to continue their conquest.

The news was indeed all bad. In February, German submarines in numbers were off the Atlantic coast and in the Caribbean. They sank ships on the very doorsills of the oil port of Aruba and in Chesapeake Bay. The Nazis had been turned back before Moscow, but the Russian army had been hit so hard that the Soviets were appealing for a landing in France at any cost to take some of the pres-

sure off them. England had barely escaped with
her life from the daylight bombings of 1940; now
every night the German bombers were over London, Coventry, Liverpool, Bristol. In Australia
the Japanense had struck at Port Darwin on the
northern coast with a crushing air raid on February 10, which smashed up all the shipping in the
harbor and so wrecked the place itself that we no
longer had a forward base from which the empire
could be attacked. Any strategic plans the United
States had were destroyed, and no new ones could
be developed in the face of the overwhelming neces-
sities of defense.

before engaging with the guns. It was a complete victory; the enemy heavy and two of his light destroyers went down, the survivor escaping only with difficulty and heavy damage.

A new strategic situation was now presented to the American command. In the north, the operation in the Aleutians was in full progress and, in Europe, that against Sicily. Both were making heavy demands for cruiser and destroyer support and, with the incapacitation of Ainsworth's ships, Merrill's was the only squadron that could be spared for operations in the Solomons. Involvement in such another siege as that of Munda, with the necessity of providing gunnery support and intercepting Japanese efforts at relief would be almost certain to produce damage to ships, whereas experience indicated that the Japanese island bases were powerless if we possessed airfields close enough to them to cut their communications. The next step therefore was not to Kolombangara for a direct attack on the Vila position, but past it to Vella Lavella Island, where the Japanese had no occupation forces to speak of.

The move was accomplished on August 15 with little fighting. On the following night the Japanese, still apparently with their minds fixed on Vila, tried to run in a big convoy of fast troop-laden barges, straight across the Slot from Choiseul Island under destroyer escort. A division of Ameri-

can destroyers drove off the escorts in a brief gunnery fight and sank most of the barges with enormous losses among the occupants. This was the last attempt to reinforce Vila, the enemy changing his plan to one of straight rear-guard fighting.

Under this new system, everything American that moved on the water was subjected to harassing air attacks, mainly at night and usually with torpedoes, after snooper planes had outlined the target with flares as in the attack on Admiral Giffen's squadron early in the year. The burden of the work afloat lay on the destroyer men, and in the air on the aviators working from fields newly won from jungle. All through August and September this type of fighting went on in a series of tiring daily battles too small to be recorded. The Japanese were gradually growing weaker, for their planes could not hold head against ours nor were their mechanics equal to the task of maintenance. The loss figures gradually mounted to approximately ten to one. During those two months the Japanese discovered that with American air bases on both sides of it, Vila was useless. They began to evacuate at night by fast barges across the Slot to Choiseul. PT-boats could accomplish little against these barges, which were both armored and heavily armed. The destroyers had to be used and were nearly always counterattacked from the air. Fortunately none was lost; and not over 5 percent of the

estimated 40,000 Japanese on Kolombangara escaped.

The question of another step forward had been that of waiting for troops and supplies, since the men who had fought at Munda needed rest. At the end of October these needs were met, and it was determined to move into the Empress Augusta Bay area of Bougainville, which would both neutralize the network of Japanese bases in the Shortlands and place their big center at Rabaul under fighter-covered attack, rendering it untenable as a harbor. The transports moved in on the night of October 30. That same night Merrill's cruisers ran out ahead to give the airfields at Buin-Faisi a shelling, and turned back to shell the Shortlands the following dawn as a means of keeping enemy planes on the ground.

The Japanese perceived the implications of the Bougainville attack at once. However willing they might be to fight rear-guard actions in the Central Solomons, this represented a threat they could not ignore. Next night, November 1, they sent down from Rabaul a squadron of four cruisers and eight destroyers to attack our transports and installations in the bay. At midnight the squadron was intercepted by Admiral Merrill with exactly the same numerical force but considerably less strength, since two of the Japanese cruisers were heavies with stout armor and eight-inch guns.

The battle was one of the most brilliant tactical performances of the whole war. Merrill flung his destroyer divisions in two flanking attacks on the Japanese as they advanced in three columns, himself with the cruisers shuttling back and forth across the head of the enemy advance, covering his torpedo attack by gunfire. After a two-hour action the enemy turned in flight; one of their cruisers and two destroyers had been sunk and all the others were more or less damaged. Merrill had suffered serious injuries to only one destroyer, hit by a torpedo.

At daybreak before the American squadron could clear the area, some 80 Japanese bombers staged down from Rabaul to attack them, but were beaten off with heavy loss and no damage to the ships. The fighting ashore had been progressing with the same dogged slowness as at the other places where Japanese were encountered in jungle, but the enemy were without prepared positions in the Empress Augusta Bay region and had difficulty getting reinforcements and supplies to the front along the narrow trails. In spite of the fanaticism of their resistance the perimeter of the landing area was steadily extended. The danger to the Rabaul base was now acute; the Japanese brought down a squadron of six heavy cruisers with lighter units to the number of 18, which were seen entering Rabaul harbor by scouts from MacArthur's com

mand on November 5, evidently for a thrust against the beachhead.

This was more than Merrill's little squadron could handle. Well off to the south to keep beyond range of enemy aerial observation, the veteran carrier *Saratoga* had been lying in the offing, accompanied by the first of a series of new light carriers built on cruiser hulls, the *Princeton*. Halsey sent them in against this new threat. They ran north all through the night and at daybreak flew out every plane they had. There was a heavy overcast at Rabaul but with plenty of visibility underneath it. The carrier planes came through this in a surprise attack, meeting almost no airborne opposition and, amid intense anti-aircraft fire, fell on the Japanese squadron. They had been instructed to neglect the usual technique of making sure of sinking a damaged ship in favor of damaging all the enemy ships sufficiently to keep them from making the run to Bougainville. This plan was followed to the letter. Out of all the ships in Rabaul harbor only one cruiser steamed away unhurt and one of the Japanese destroyers was sunk. The following morning our scouts found Rabaul empty, the whole fleet turned back to Truk to lick its wounds.

This did not end Japanese efforts to inflict a serious blow on the beachheads. They began staging in planes in considerable quantities, and by No-

vember 10 had so many at Rabaul as to make operations difficult for our scouts. On the morning of the 11th, Halsey sent his two carriers back in from the south, while down from the Central Pacific to the region east of Rabaul came three new carriers—*Essex, Bunker Hill, Independence*—under Rear-Admiral Montgomery, which also flew out airplanes for a strike. The weather was very bad, with fog and rain, and the results at Rabaul were by no means all that could have been hoped for. But Japanese snooper planes had traced Montgomery's attackers back to his ships and the air squadrons that should have gone to Empress Augusta Bay were flown off in a great blow against the fleet instead.

Since the outbreak of the war a vast naval-aviation training program had been in progress in America, carried on with unhurrying thoroughness in spite of the time pressure. Of the new pilots produced these new carriers had the best. The air battle that followed was less a combat than a mass execution. When our land-based planes from Vella Lavella arrived in response to calls from the fleet, they found undamaged ships and over 60 Japanese planes burning on the water. They shot down 24 more planes during the enemy's retreat, and now the planned Japanese attack at Bougainville could not be delivered. This was their last attempt at a serious effort to relieve the pressure.

THE presence of Montgomery's new carriers in the brief Rabaul raid and the shortage of cruisers that made Merrill's squadron the sole support of the Bougainville expedition were effects from the same cause. After the Kula Gulf actions and the attacks in the Aleutians in the summer of 1943, it became clear that the Japanese had no further intention of risking major fleet units in defense of outposts at the perimeter of their empire. Our chiefs therefore began to consider an offensive on an oceanic scale— one which would either force the enemy into a major battle or make him give up bases to our use.

In oceanic terms the Japanese positions in the Gilberts now formed a salient; to defend them his fleet would have to venture as far from any base where damaged ships could be repaired after an action as would our own from Pearl Harbor. The enemy would thus be forced to fight us on equal terms; and battle on any terms near equality was now ardently desired by our command. The completion of our six new battleships and the enemy's losses off Guadalcanal had swung the balance on the gunnery line heavily in the direction of the American fleet, and the Japanese carrier force was known to have been cut to pieces.

There remained the land-based planes of the "unsinkable carriers" of the islands; but the use of these, a fundamental basis of Japanese strategy, contained a fallacy. The airplane could indeed

move faster than any ship; but by loading planes on carrier decks it should be possible to assemble at a chosen point of impact a force of planes sufficient to overwhelm anything the local defensive resources could send up, while the strategic mobility of the fighting planes—the ability to cover long distances—was so limited that it could be brought to a combat area by ship far more quickly than it could be flown in. One of the defects of the Japanese air campaign for Guadalcanal had been precisely that their policy of piecemeal reinforcement had brought them nothing but piecemeal losses.

The date of the new campaign thus had to be set for a time when we would have carrier strength sufficient to break the local air forces in the Gilberts; and that date was set for the last days of November. At that time three large and some seven light carriers should be assembled with eight or nine escort carriers, which were now flowing from the yards at the rate of three or four a month. They were organized in groups like Montgomery's, each a semi-autonomous organization with gunnery ships in support. The force of fast battleships cruised with the whole. The old slow battleships were to furnish gunnery support at the beaches keeping the escort carriers under guard while these latter gave close support to the troops ashore. The troops of the 27th Army Division were to fall on Makin Island while the 2nd Marine Division

was assigned the island of Tarawa. Nearly three months of special training was given these landing forces.

Preliminary bombardments were begun several days before landing time, and the island was combed both with shells and gunfire for every defensive installation that had been revealed by a careful study of aerial photographs. On November 20 the double attack started with extensive use of the new types of landing vessels, for the first time in the Pacific.

At Makin a preliminary bombardment had achieved everything that could be desired. The 300 defenders left alive were stunned by shellfire and made but poor resistance. But Tarawa was more difficult. It had been fortified to an extent unrevealed by the photographs, with enormous and deep concrete dugouts roofed in steel, which resisted all bombardment. An error had been made in the preliminary timetable so that fire from the ships was lifted 40 minutes before the Marines reached the beaches, and the Japanese were given the opportunity to come out of their dugouts into firing positions. Inaccurate preliminary information from former residents about the height of the offshore reef at the prevailing tide had the result that many of the landing craft hung on it, under fire and losing heavily. By twilight of the first day the Marines were clinging desperately to a single small strip of

beach and part of a ruined pier. It seemed not unlikely that they would be thrown back into the sea.

Under the personal leadership of Major-General
Holland Smith they pressed on nevertheless, while
destroyers came inshore to give fire support, and
planes from all the carriers lent their aid. The
concrete bunkers proved impervious alike to shells
and bombs. The island had to be taken inch by
inch, each bunker carried in a separate military
operation by means of flame throwers, grenades,
and explosive charges. The conquest took four days
and the casualties were over 2,900, more than a
quarter of the Marines engaged. On the last day
of the fighting ashore an escort carrier in the offing
was torpedoed by a Japanese submarine, and blew
up with nearly all hands.

A thrill of horror went through the country as
this news from the Pacific followed so closely on
that of desperate fighting in Italy for results that
bulked so small on the map. The Russian counter-
offensive seemed stalled; among the Solomons a
new cruiser division had appeared to join Merrill's,
but two of its ships were hit by Japanese torpedo
planes on the first night patrol, and it seemed that
the Allies like the Axis might be unable to drive
an offensive home without ruinous cost.

CHAPTER X

THE ISLAND CHAIN BROKEN

THE last Japanese troops at Buna and Gona were exterminated in January, 1943. At this time the enemy were still convinced that they could defend their empire with a hard crust of positions around its borders, using airplanes as the binding material and making a campaign as toilsome as that for Guadalcanal necessary for the capture of each position. They themselves expected to avoid their former error of wasting their mobile sea forces in the defense.

There was some reason in their viewpoint. It had taken us six months to gain control of that bloody Solomon Island, and it was only an isolated outpost, whereas the new network of positions in the south ran in a great semicircle of mutual support from Lae and Salamaua on Huon Gulf of New Guinea through New Britain down to the Munda-Vila complex in the Central Solomons. The planes from its fields made impossible any American naval effort in the sea thus enclosed.

While General MacArthur's men were laboriously consolidating the Buna-Gona position by means of men and materials taken forward by air and while Admiral Halsey's forces were preparing for their step forward into the Russell Islands, the Japanese were reinforcing the bases from which they hoped to seal off our gains. We have seen how they moved forces into the Central Solomons. At the same time they decided to put enough troops into Lae, Salamaua, and Finschaffen to make them secure against anything but an attack of the most serious character. These bases controlled Vitiaz Strait and hence access to the waters north of New Guinea.

A convoy of not less than twelve large and fast transports was assembled at Rabaul with something like two full divisions of troops aboard and a division of big destroyers for escort. On March 1, when the weather presented a favorable opportunity, with a heavy cloud and storm front running down the latitudes toward New Guinea, the expedition put out.

The preparations had been no secret from our side; in fact, one of our submarines sank a destroyer of the escort while the convoy was gathering. General George C. Kenney, commander of MacArthur's air force, had all his planes ready—somewhere around 100 of the heavy bombers which could operate at so great a distance from base. He had

lately discovered that a bomb dropped by such a plane while in level flight low over the water would skip like a stone skimmed across a pond, and had been training his fliers to use this as a bombing method. As soon as the convoy was well at sea he threw his entire force upon it. The Japanese had some fighter cover but these planes were gravely hampered by the weather and still more by the tactics of the Americans, since a fighter attempting to dive upon a bomber which is at wave-top level almost invariably crashes in the sea.

The new skip-bombing technique succeeded even beyond expectations, especially since the ships practiced the normal tactic of swinging broadside to the direction of the attack to prevent the bombers running the length of their decks. Five-hundred-pound bombs plunged right in through the thin sides of transports and escorting vessels alike, exploding in the engine rooms and along the water line. By the close of the first day several ships had gone down and one had beached herself on the coast of New Britain. The rest scattered and pressed on in accordance with the Japanese doctrine of never abandoning an operation once begun, but the following morning the bombers were after them again and on March 3 were still hammering those that remained. Not one of the Japanese ships reached port, and scarcely a man

ever got to shore. The disaster was so complete that General MacArthur afterward called it the decisive battle of the whole Pacific war. While it hardly merits that description, the clash in the Bismarck Sea certainly exercised a severe restrictive influence on Japanese strategy from this point forward. Never again did they attempt to move bodies of troops across open water in regions where our air power could be brought to bear.

As soon as this fact was apprehended, American South Pacific strategy was greatly simplified. It was not necessary to conduct a full campaign against each of the Japanese strong points. For an advance toward the sources of their power, it was only necessary to seize similar points among the islands ourselves and from the airfields installed at these places to provide cover for traffic moving by sea. The enemy installations could be neglected; the men in them might continue to exist on the "bounty of the tropics," but without air or sea assistance they could undertake no offensive operations. This was essentially the same conclusion that had been arrived at among the Solomons by a somewhat different line of reasoning. From the fact that the subsequent campaign was described as one of encirclements, it seems to have owed something to the strategy of land warfare as practiced by the great armies of Germany and Russia, with whom it had become normal practice to pene-

trate a front, then isolate an enemy groupment to be mopped up more or less at leisure later.

The first fruit of this new strategy was the occupation of the Kiriwina and Woodlark Islands, north of the eastern tip of New Guinea, on June 22–23; where nothing beyond enemy signal stations was found. The intervening time had been spent in resting and reorganizing the troops who had fought so hard at Buna-Gona in a slow advance westward along the New Guinea shore from these places toward Lae and Salamaua and clearing up the aerial situation. The Japanese apparently regarded MacArthur's forward move as even more of a menace than the campaign in the Solomons, and they made persistent efforts to lame it by the same means they had used there. All through April and May they continued their harassing air attacks and though, as in the Solomons, their losses were severe, it was not until the Kiriwina-Woodlark operation, with the arrival of planes to use the air strip set up there, that our forces could gain air cover enough to move convoys with impunity around the eastern capes of Papua.

In the spring of 1943 an Australian force had been working toilsomely through the jungles of the Owen Stanley Mountains, well westward of the Moresby-Buna pass. By mid-August both this force and that which had been moving along the coast were

in position for an attack on Lae and Salamaua. Heavy raids were flown against the Japanese supporting air bases at Wewak and Medang to keep enemy planes from interfering. Destroyers moved in to give gunnery support and the assault on Salamaua began on August 19. Although the Japanese resistance was not particularly strong in firepower, progress at first was slow despite the help of amphibian forces which landed on the beach south of the place.

General MacArthur accordingly made a rapid shift of strategy. A parachute force was dropped at Nadzab in the open Markham Valley northwest of Lae, where it successfully seized the airfield

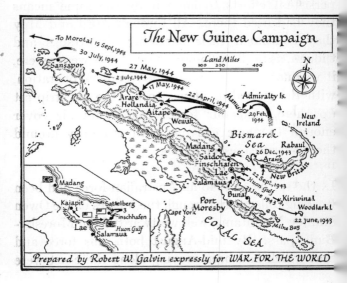

The New Guinea Campaign

Land Miles

To Morotai 15 Sept, 1944
30 July, 1944
Sansapor
27 May, 1944
2 July, 1944
17 May, 1944
22 April, 1944
Admiralty Is.
Arare
Hollandia
Aitape
Wewak
29 Feb. 1944
New Ireland
Bismarck Sea
Madang
Saidor
26 Dec., 1943
Rabaul
Finschhafen
22 Sept. 1943
Arawe
Lae
New Britain
Salamaua
Huon Gulf
Buna
30 June 1943
Kiriwina I.
Madang
Port Moresby
Woodlark I.
Kaiapit
Sattelberg
22 June, 1943
Finschhafen
Cape York
Milne Bay
Lae
Huon Gulf
Salamaua
CORAL SEA

Prepared by Robert W. Galvin expressly for WAR FOR THE WORLD

making room for an entire Australian airborne division which was quickly flown in. The whole Lae-Salamaua area was now cut off, and in the early days of September a concentric attack on the double position was launched. It broke through in all directions and both places were occupied by September 16. Once more there were scarcely any prisoners. The rather surprising feebleness of the defense was found to be due to the complete failure of the Japanese medical service in coping with tropical diseases, especially malaria and beriberi, which had so enfeebled the garrisons that they were in need of relief as far back as the date of the battle of the Bismarck Sea.

Finschaffen was immediately attacked by amphibious forces and was in our possession by October 2, but both from this point and from Lae a good many of the Japanese escaped to the mountain jungles of the Huon Peninsula, where they assembled on a high plateau called the Sattelburg. From this point they conducted operations well above the guerrilla level and the advance had to be halted until they were eliminated. But while this cleanup was going on, Halsey's forces got ashore at Empress Augusta Bay on Bougainville. A short time later the air strips there made it possible to keep American fighter planes over Rabaul. That struck the death knell of the great Japanese base; its fields were now untenable for aircraft and its

harbor for shipping; and with the elimination of Rabaul the whole circle of Japanese outer defenses in the south fell apart.

Late in November the Japanese began running destroyers (a Tokyo Express in reverse) down to Kahili and the Buin-Faisi fields to evacuate the technical personnel of whom they had so few that every man was valuable. One of these groups was intercepted on the night of November 25 by Captain Arleigh Burke with the destroyers of the famous "Little Beaver" squadron off St. George's Channel, and in a hot little engagement he sank three of the six Japanese destroyers present without losing a man.

This substantially ended Japanese efforts to get men out of the Solomons, as similar previous actions had ended their efforts to move them in. The American advance now went on. On December 1 a strong force was thrown ashore at Arawe on the southern coast of New Britain itself, finding practically no opposition and speedily setting up a new forward base there. The way through Vitiaz Strait was now open; toward the end of the month the 32nd Division was landed on the north shore of Huon Peninsula and joined in eliminating the Satelburg Japanese, who had been under heavy attack from two Australian divisions and who were beginning to break up at this time. The process was not accomplished without heavy fighting and some

losses, but it was slow and difficult rather than
dangerous in a military sense, as the Japanese had
no prepared positions.

Harder fighting followed on December 26 when
the 1st Marine Division was pushed through
Vitiaz Strait to seize Long Island at its western
end and to land on both sides of the Cape Gloucester Peninsula on the northern shore of New Britain.
A small force had also worked through the mountains from Arawe to support this attack from the
landward side. An important Japanese air station
at Cape Gloucester formed the link between their
air bases at Rabaul and Kavieng and one held by
them at Wewak on the New Guinea coast. The
place was accordingly heavily defended. Moreover, the preliminary aerial bombardment had
failed to neutralize the Japanese field, though it
was the heaviest air attack yet made in the Southwest Pacific—360 tons of bombs were dropped.
In an air battle of considerable intensity the Japanese lost 61 planes; we lost seven, and several of
our ships were hit.

On December 30 the Marines carried the airfield
in a rush, but were brought up short before a hill
behind an extensive swamp, where the enemy had
dug themselves in around their artillery positions
and had filled the trees with snipers. A ten-day
battle was required to win the eminence; it was
featured by the ingenuity of our engineers in get-

ting troops across the swamp on foot bridges slung from trees.

Despite raids by American destroyers, the Japanese had been using Kavieng on New Ireland as an air base for the area ever since Rabaul came under attack from the bombers at Bougainville. The Cape Gloucester field brought both that point and Wewak under persistent fighter-covered attack and rendered any sustained operations by the enemy impossible. But the task of neutralizing the Japanese bases in the south was not really completed until February 16, 1944, when, supported by the cruisers from the Solomons, the 1st Cavalry Division was put ashore on Green Island close up to Rabaul and two weeks later on Los Negros Island in the Admiralty group.

The way was now clear for MacArthur's advance westward along the coast of New Guinea. One of his flanks was covered by the impassable jungles of the central part of the island, the other by open ocean. The Japanese might indeed bring their fleet into action across this ocean, but it was now alive with American cruiser, aerial, and submarine patrols, and our own fast striking forces hovered in the offing nearer to the central scene of action than were the Japanese from any concentration point they still had in operation. General MacArthur's strategy had thus far scored a complete success. His own losses were less than one to ten of

the enemy's. He had thrown his bases so far forward that his own long-range bombers were attacking enemy posts in the Dutch Indies and he had cut off and pushed completely out of the war in their now-useless garrison posts a number of Japanese nearly equal to his entire army, some of the best troops in the empire.

These Japanese did not remain altogether quiescent; there was continual obscure fighting on a small scale along the approaches to Medang, on New Britain and Bougainville. But the ingenious American General turned even this to advantage by sending to these areas troops freshly arrived from the States or Australia to gain jungle-fighting experience under conditions in which they could be given so great a superiority in numbers, firepower, and air cover that their casualties were always light.

ONE of the reasons why it had been possible in February, 1944, to move up to the Admiralty Islands, a point seemingly caught between the great Japanese bases of Kavieng and Truk, was that the enemy was so deeply occupied elsewhere. During the Makin-Tarawa attacks our fleet had received the constant attention of Japanese torpedo planes, always coming in at twilight, partly from the fields in the Marshalls and partly from the lonely island of Nauru. During the Gilberts

operation they hit one of the carriers, not sinking her indeed, but sending her back for a long period in dock. As soon as Tarawa was secure, in the early days of September, 1943, Admiral Lee ran down with the fast battleships and subjected Nauru to an intense surprise shelling that effectively ruined it as a base, since the Japanese had no means of replacing lost personnel and shop facilities without advancing their fleet.

For the Marshalls another method of neutralization was intended; they were the next point of attack on the line of the Central Pacific offensive that was to be conducted parallel with General MacArthur's movement along the coast of New Guinea. This island group was a widespread one, covering ten degrees of latitude and 15 of longitude, nearly as much as the Philippines, but the areas of land are very small, consisting of narrow coralline atolls encircling lagoons. No island is more than a mile or two wide. These lagoons make admirable sheltered harbors; the islands themselves need only to be cleared of some of their vegetation to become air strips.

The Japanese had been twenty years in the Marshall group, and reconnaissance photograph showed air strips on all the more important atolls If the experience at Tarawa were any criterion the places were formidably fortified. There was als a strong possibility that an attack on the Marshall

might bring the Japanese fleet out for a showdown fight. The island group did not constitute an outpost of empire that could be sacrificed in return for attrition among the attacking forces; it was part of the main imperial defensive system, linking up with the Carolines and Truk.

If the Japanese fleet came, our own would be hampered by the presence of the transports which it dared not leave, so the enemy could choose the time, place, and manner of attack. If our strength in carriers was now very great, it would be at least partly negated by the fact that from his numerous strips among the islands the enemy should be able to concentrate more land-based planes than had yet opposed any of our forward moves.

It was toward the weakening of these local air forces that the first efforts of the attackers were directed. As soon as the Tarawa air strip was prepared for use, long-range army Liberators and navy Venturas were brought in, and beginning on December 22, 1943, treated the whole Marshall group to a systematic pounding, with special attention to shops and fuel dumps. Between that date and January 30, Milli was thus visited 12 times, Jaluit 10, Kwajalein 8, Wotje 7, Maloelap 9, and Kusaie, the staging field in the Eastern Carolines, twice, all with heavy raids. At all these points lusty anti-aircraft fire was encountered, but fighter opposition was comparatively light and showed a tendency to

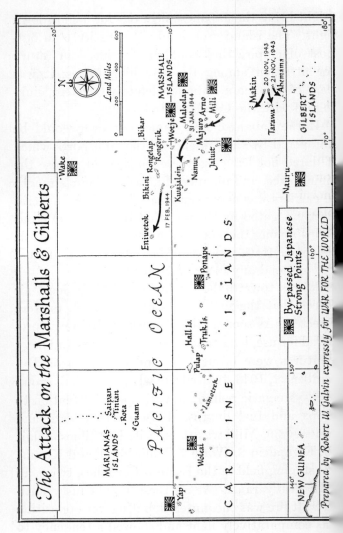

The Attack on the Marshalls & Gilberts

MARIANAS ISLANDS
Saipan
Tinian
Rota
Guam

Yap

Woleai

Ulithi
Lamotrek

Pulap
Hall Is.
Truk Is.

Ponape

CAROLINE   ISLANDS

PACIFIC OCEAN

Wake

Eniwetok
17 FEB. 1944

Bikini Rongelap
Rongerik

Kwajalein
Namur

MARSHALL
ISLANDS

Wotje
Maloelap
31 JAN. 1944

Majuro Arno
Jaluit
Mili

Bikar

Nauru

Makin
20 NOV. 1943
Tarawa 21 NOV. 1943
Abemama

GILBERT
ISLANDS

By-passed Japanese
Strong Points

N

Land Miles
0   200   400   600

Prepared by Robert W Galvin expressly for WAR FOR THE WORLD

decrease. There was no sign of any Japanese ships
except submarines.

On January 30, fleet operations under the command of Admiral Spruance began with a violent
simultaneous attack from the planes of three carrier groups (a carrier group normally contained
two large and two small carriers, though not invariably) against the islands of Kwajalein atoll,
while from escort carriers in the rear other planes
joined the land-based craft. On the following
morning the battleships were up and helped the
planes of two carrier groups in another attack on
Kwajalein which was to be the point of the landing. This was a complete surprise to the Japanese,
who had expected our forces indeed, but against
some atoll much farther east. Admiral F. C. Sherman's carrier group went on for a strike against
Eniwetok, the most remote of the Marshalls and
beyond the reach of land-based bombers from
Tarawa.

Kwajalein atoll is shaped somewhat like a bent
banana. At the bend is Roi, the most important
island. Kwajalein Island itself is at the southern
tip of the atoll. These two spots received the brunt
of the attack. During the afternoon and evening
of the first strike there was a good deal of air
fighting around Roi but the carrier fighter group
had so well disposed of Japanese scouts that local
as well as strategic surprise was secured and most

of their planes were destroyed on the ground. They attempted the usual torpedo-plane attacks against our fleet in the twilight but with little success, and on the morning of February 2, under gunnery cover from the old, slow battleships, the troops began to land. The 4th Marine Division attacked Roi, the 7th Army Division Kwajalein. Just after the first wave reached the shore at Roi, the battleship *Colorado* scored a direct hit on the island's main ammunition dump, which blew up with one of the most violent explosions ever seen in the Pacific.

The Japanese resisted with their usual fanaticism, but most had been stunned or killed by the explosion and what preceded it. Before night the island was American except for a few snipers. At Kwajalein the supporting fire was similarly effective and though the conquest took two days, this was mainly because it became a problem of digging the shell-shocked defenders out of the underground retreats where they had hidden themselves. Majuro atoll was occupied without resistance.

Eniwetok was scheduled to be attacked next— its possession would cut off the eastern Marshalls from Japan and would give us a valuable forward base—but the troop convoys for it were still distant and the fast carrier force of Spruance with its attack battleships was for the moment unemployed. Submarine scouts had reported heavy Japanese ships in the neighborhood of Truk. The Admiral

decided to run down for an attack on that place
on the chance of persuading the enemy to battle.
It is not easy to convey the feeling in the fleet
when the news of where they were bound spread
among the ships. Truk was the Japanese Pearl Harbor, a legend and a mystery in the fleet during a
generation in which no white man had been allowed
to visit the place. Its strength was supposed to be
immense, its defensive installations the best in the
world.

Elaborate precautions were taken and elaborate
tactical plans worked out, but they proved unnecessary. The Japanese fleet had fled Truk, and
when our fighter planes, far in advance of the ships,
swept over the great fortress on the morning of
February 17 they found no major ships, but scores
of Japanese fighters shooting past them into the
spotty clouds to gain altitude for diving counterattacks. There was an air battle distinguished by
the fact that only fighters were engaged on both
sides; the Japanese lost 127 planes shot down, we
lost eighteen. Then the dive and torpedo bombers
came in for attacks on the shore positions and
shipping. The operation lasted two full days; on
the evening of the second day a Japanese torpedo
plane got a hit on an American carrier but the
enemy had paid for that with 23 ships sunk, five
of them warships, and the loss of 204 planes. The
Truk bogey had been fully exorcised.

Spruance swung his ships back to the north and two days later raided the Marianas, where he sank more ships, mostly small, establishing the fact that the Japanese fleet was not making a wide sweep round by the north to interfere with operations in the Marshalls. Away behind Spruance the big *Saratoga* and the escort carriers had now been pounding Eniwetok for days with the help of cruiser divisions. On February 18, the same day that saw the end of the actions against Truk, Marines were set on the beaches there. The Eniwetok operation was not quite as perfect as the Kwajalein attack but came close to it. In two days the atoll was ours at the cost of 500 casualties. The whole outer barrier of Japanese defense had been broken down; Truk was effectively out of the war; and the radical defect in the Japanese system of island-based airpower had been found—that from their scattered stations the enemy could achieve nowhere near enough aerial concentration to deal with a fleet that came up out of the ocean with twenty carriers in line.

CHAPTER XI

DOMINATING the hill road through Cassino in central Italy was a monastery of great antiquity and beauty. The Germans had converted the area into a fortress and observation post which enabled their artillery, now well dug in, to come down with great accuracy on any movement from our side, while the Allied forces lacked similar aids. The position had to be won before the advance on Rome could proceed through the central valleys. For his operation of January, 1944, General Alexander planned a complex double attack to achieve the desired result.

Two British divisions were to cross the lower Garigliano and, swinging north, force the small Liri River, which flows into the Garigliano at right angles just at Cassino. The American 36th Division was to assault the line in front while a French corps was working through the mountains north of Cassino for a swing southward, similar to that

being made by the British from the opposite direction. It was a double penetration to be followed by a double envelopment of the position.

Meanwhile the American VI Corps (actually only half of it was American) had been taken out of line. It would be landed from the sea on the beaches of the summer resort at Anzio-Nettuno, some thirty-five miles south of Rome. Difficulties with communications, caused chiefly by Allied aerial operations, had forced the Germans into some rather eccentric dispositions; it was hoped and expected that this triple attack would at one point or another find them unable to support a position before it could be broken through.

The British began their attack on January 17; they forced the Garigliano but were halted as they attempted to make the wheel northward. The attack of the American 36th failed under heavy losses, and though the French among the high Apennines worked through the German defensive system, no more than the British could they make the necessary wheel. The Cassino position held in spite of some local gains by the American 34th Division, which was moved into line when the 36th was driven back.

The Anzio force struck on January 22. It achieved fairly easy initial success but General Clark, in command, mindful of the difficulties at Salerno, waited for some time to get heavy equip-

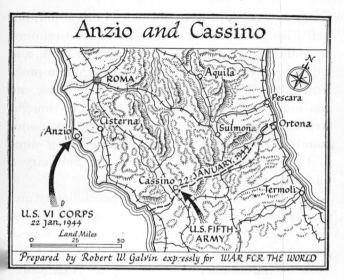

Anzio *and* Cassino

U.S. VI CORPS
22 Jan., 1944

Land Miles

U.S. FIFTH ARMY

Prepared by Robert W. Galvin expressly for WAR FOR THE WORLD

ment and tanks ashore, meanwhile confining his activities to patrols. At the end of three days the Germans had not only recovered from their surprise but also they had beaten back the 36th Division in the south and brought the British to a halt. They rushed in all their reserves, including much armor, cut the drainage dikes of what had once been a system of swamps, and from dominating hills in the rear opened a terrific fire both on the beaches and the supporting ships. An improved type of glider bomb was also directed at everything that moved on the water, with the design of cutting the beachhead units from their support.

The hopeful offensive was changed to desperate

defense. The ships were not indeed driven off, but a British battleship was heavily hit, two cruisers, several destroyers and smaller craft were sunk, and supplies on the beachhead rapidly became a problem. Everything in the area was under intense and continuous artillery fire. The Germans thought well enough of their chances to launch two major counterattacks with six divisions, including some of their best armored formations, on February 9 and February 17.

The first was beaten off with great difficulty and somewhat constricted the already narrow area of the beachhead. By the date of the second, a fresh American division (the 45th) had reached the shore with a number of British tanks. A defensive perimeter was organized and held, along the lines of some canals. The Germans themselves had suffered considerable losses, particularly from Allied aviation, and it required all the troops of their tactical reserve to maintain the various and complicated positions along the lines now existing. But they were holding, and an important difficulty had begun to develop on our side, where the casualties had been far above expectations and the flow of replacements far below. The difficulty arose in part from the failure of the Selective Service System to meet the army's requirements in manpower in part, from the army itself, which had overmanned such formations as air force ground crews

military police, supply corps and headquarters paper-work units, while undersupplying the combat infantry to a precisely equal extent.

THE next attempt to break through the Cassino position came in March, 1944, and was an effort to make use of the growing Allied superiority in the air. The ancient monastery on the hill had thus far been spared because of its religious significance, but as Allied forces inched forward on both sides it became clear that the building was the key of the whole position. It was therefore announced that it would be bombed. On March 22, Allied planes working in relays gave the place the heaviest bombardment any spot of similar size had ever received. The monastery was reduced to rubble and the ground around it torn to pieces, but when our infantry came forward toward evening they found so many Germans holding out in the ruins that the attack could not be pressed home. The bombing, like the days of drumfire to which Western front positions were subjected in 1916, had only succeeded in tearing up the ground so that neither supplies nor artillery could be brought forward.

After this failure, there was a long period of quiescence, during which the Fifth and Eighth armies were regrouped and new troops brought in, while the air forces hammered unremittingly at German

communications and produced a gradual weakening in ways that were not at once apparent. The Anzio beachhead was gradually reinforced till it contained three American and two British infantry divisions, an American armored division, and various special groups amounting to another division in strength, the whole under the command of Major General Lucian K. Truscott. Two fresh American divisions were placed on the Appian Way front of the Garigliano line; the British Eighth Army, reinforced by Polish troops, took over the whole sector from the Adriatic to below Cassino.

The new plan was for the Eighth Army to sweep round the lofty summit of Mt. Tyro behind Cassino and get down into the upper reaches of the Liri valley, while the Fifth attacked by its left along the shore with naval help, and Truscott's men broke out of their beachhead. The German forces were now commanded by Marshal Von Kesselring; they had some twelve divisions in line on the southern front with five more surrounding the Anzio beachhead and another eight in army reserve. But most of these divisions were under strength, so the Allies possessed somewhat the superior forces. Moreover, Allied air superiority had become overpowering, and in Italy, at least, transportation had been recognized as the major German weakness. Our planes had bombed out every railroad yard and nearly every bridge below

Florence before the attack opened on May 11 all along the line.

Truscott delayed for a brief time to induce the Germans to send as many men as possible to their southern front. Among the hills the French and British got through, and on May 16 Cassino fell with 1,500 prisoners, while along the coast the green American division made steady if somewhat slow progress. By the 20th the Eighth Army was making good advances up the main road through Cassino and it became apparent that the Germans were withdrawing—it was supposed to another system of defenses called "The Hitler Line," which had been much spoken of.

On the 23rd General Truscott launched his attack—the British elements driving straight toward Rome, while the American attacked northeast towards Cisterna on the Appian Way, which had been the objective point of the beachhead fighting. Von Kesselring had pulled his artillery back in anticipation of such a move and made an extremely good defense, holding tightly to the key communication centers on the two main roads—Velletri and Valmontane—until he extricated the bulk of his formations. The chief gains along the ground were thus merely territorial, but this warfare of movement forced the Nazis to use the roads even by daylight; they lost heavily to the Allied air forces in the process and were now unable to find a stabi-

lizing position in the Alban hills anywhere south
of Rome. On June 2 the Velletri-Valmontane line
was broken when infantry scaled the summit between the two towns, and on June 4 Allied columns were marching into Rome.

From this point the roads fan out in several directions. The pursuers followed close on the Germans,
who were in some disorder, and the prospect of
following still more vigorously to convert the retreat into a rout must have been an attractive one.
But over-all strategic considerations intervened.
When Rome fell, the scheduled invasion of northern France was only twenty-four hours away and
it was essential to prepare for the support of this
operation by an attack through southern France
with a reconstituted Seventh Army and French
forces. In mid-June three American and four
French divisions were taken out of line to prepare
for this operation, being replaced by fewer and
less-experienced troops.

Moreover, our men were now advancing through
the country where roads and bridges had been dev-
astated by our air forces, to which the Germans
had added by demolitions carried out with their
usual skill, so that as the lines lengthened supply
became a serious problem. The drive slowed. In
mid-July the Germans made a stout defense before
the important port of Leghorn, which had to be
taken by an encirclement from the east after a pre-

liminary operation had gained heights for artillery support. By the end of that same month the Germans were back to the Arno River, which is deep and wide; the heights on its north bank afforded them the artillery observation posts they knew so well how to use. Here the position stabilized.

THE submarine war had really been won in 1943; Admiral King issued a statement in March of 1944 which honestly said that these raiders had been changed from menace to problem. By this time the new types of torpedoes had been thoroughly mastered; destroyer escorts and escort carriers were appearing in such numbers that it was possible to give every convoy the opulent cover that had hitherto been provided only for a few of great importance. There was no longer any real hindrance in the flow of troops and supplies to Europe, a fact which aided immeasurably in planning the land operations there.

Moreover, the German order for submarines to fight matters out with planes had by this time brought unmitigated disaster upon the U-boat service. The plane-borne depth charge had been improved to a point where it was very deadly, and, given an aviator's ability to see a submarine some distance under the surface, the step of ordering them to fight planes might seem necessary. But once on the surface the submarine had no weapons

that could cope with the gunpower of destroyers and destroyer escorts, which now invariably appeared soon after a plane had made contact.

The losses in these hopeless battles against the combined Allied forces almost invariably fell on the ablest and boldest submarine captains, those who most fully carried out the orders to stand and fight. The result was a perceptible break in the morale of the whole service at some time in 1944. Careful Nazi indoctrination prevented it from becoming a mutiny as a similar break had been in the previous war; but it was remarked that the U-boats had lost the spirit of the offensive. They waited for the opportunities provided by a crippled ship or a badly maneuvering convoy, returned from cruises with full loads of torpedoes, or fired them off uselessly and reported sinkings they had not made. In 1942 the German announcements of Allied tonnage sunk, compiled from submarine commanders' reports, had been within measurable distance of the facts, but in the middle of 1943 there began to be a considerable divergence, and by the end of another year, facts and German figures no longer bore any relation to each other.

The progress of a form of war in which individual battles were only incidents is perhaps best indicated statistically. In 1942 the Germans had lost 65 submarines, in return for which they sank 8,240,000 tons of shipping, or 97,059 tons for every

submarine lost. In 1943, 237 submarines went down, but got only 3,611,000 tons of ships, 15,198 tons for each submarine. By 1944 the figures were 241 submarines sunk and only 1,422,000 tons of shipping, an average of 5,900 tons per U-boat lost. In the last year the majority of the ships plying the ocean were well over 5,900 tons in size, which means that Germany was paying more than one submarine for every ship sunk. At this rate the U-boat war was not an asset but a military liability.

Not so with the American submarine war against Japan. After the first burst of energy during the Singapore-Java campaign, when Allied underwater craft could operate from bases near at hand against large military convoys, there had been a falling off. The American submarine service was not a large one at the time. The boats, based on Australia, Midway, or the Aleutians, had long distances to go and many of them were required to abstain from offensive operations to conduct necessary scouting against the movements of the Japanese fleet. In mid-1943 the Japanese also introduced a new type of depth charge which caused us some losses.

But these losses were counted in ones and twos instead of the tens and twenties of the Germans, and by that time the American submarines had already made such serious inroads on the Japanese merchant marine that its gains since the beginning of the war by new construction and capture were

entirely canceled. At least three factors contributed
to this success. Vast though the Pacific is, the
productive areas from which Japanese shipping
operated were relatively few in number; currents
and chains of reefs made the possible steaming
routes still more limited—there was no such variety of choice possible as in the open Atlantic. Sec-
ondly, the Japanese proved inefficient antisubmarine men, few of them having the technical skills
necessary for the construction and operation of such
devices as radar and supersonic gear, to which they
added the psychologically bad quality of tending to
fall into a panic or a temper at moments of stress.

The third and probably the determining cause
lay within the American submarine service itself,
an organization composed entirely of volunteers,
who were admitted only after the most searching
physical and mental examinations. Even under the
pressure of war, no short-cuts in their training were
permitted and great attention was given both to
the comfort of the men while aboard and to adequate recreation while ashore after the long cruises
—a sharp variation from the German practice.
American submarines were also much helped by the
improved radar and sound gear that began to ap-
pear in our boats, and late in 1943 by a new torpedo of great explosive power. As submarines
poured from the yards (193 were commissioned in
1942–1944, a figure small beside the German but

in total tonnage not so much less, since American submarines were nearly twice as large as theirs), their depredations became so serious as to affect the whole of Japanese strategy and economy.

The figures are somewhat approximate, since many Japanese ships were lost to mines and various combinations of submarines with other vessels, but as nearly as they can be determined they show that in 1943 American submarines sank 284 Japanese ships of 1,342,000 tons; in 1944, 492 ships of 2,388,000 tons, or nearly double the Allied shipping sunk by German submarines in the latter year. This far exceeded the Japanese replacement capacity and caused their national food rations, already at a subsistence level, to be reduced nearly a quarter. In the summer of 1944 a shortage of gasoline for even the most essential military purposes began to develop, since all Japanese oil had to come from the conquered lands to the south. Their program of general navy construction had already been constricted to provide more carriers; now many of the remaining ships were canceled in order to find steel for destroyers and other escort craft.

Even this proved insufficient. American submarines attacked not only the Japanese convoys but also their escorts, with great success. Down to the middle of 1944, American submarines had sunk some thirty Japanese destroyers, four light cruisers and one heavy, and two of the four escort carriers

Japan had managed to place in operation. Later the remaining escort carriers were sunk, with four large fleet carriers and a battleship. Submarines accounted for a total of 1,944 merchant craft, two thirds of all Japan had.

IT was the operations of the submarines quite as much as anything that led to one of the most curious campaigns of the war. When the Japanese conquered Burma early in 1942 and brought their frontier up to the Assam Mountains that separate that country from India, they effectively isolated China from the Western Allies. China had no oil within her borders nor a munitions industry capable of producing anything beyond small arms. She had already been fighting for years and her armies had been reduced to something like guerrillas. Her collapse would place such vast resources in the hands of the Japanese that it was considered essential to do something for her. The problem was not so much strictly a military one as one of engineering.

General Joseph H. Stilwell, "Vinegar Joe," a forthright, energetic, and unconventional soldier, had been sent to eastern India at the outbreak of the war and had participated in the retreat from Burma. Major-General Claire Chennault, who had recruited a group of American fliers for service with the Chinese on a mercenary basis before Pear

Harbor, was commissioned into the American air force. The first operation was to set up an aerial ferry over "the hump" of the Himalayas for absolutely essential materials. The second was to establish the 14th Air Force under General Chennault's command, operating from bases in South China. This force gave some support to China and greatly harassed the Japanese, though the amount of material damage done was small because of the difficulty of flying supplies in. At the same time the returning ferry planes brought out a number of Chinese soldiers who were trained under Stilwell's command with American arms and weapons. These men, in conjunction with the British Indian Army and a minute American expeditionary force, succeeded in 1943 in winning back part of northern Burma. Across this area, American engineers and Chinese labor began constructing a road with a parallel pipeline right through the heart of the mountains, one of the most gigantic engineering projects ever undertaken. The road ("Ledo Road," later "Stilwell Road") was not finished till late in 1944, but the Air Transport Command increased rapidly in efficiency and by June of that year was able to support another project.

This was the bombardment of the Japanese homeland and the steel factories in Manchuria. After difficulties and many delays American engineers had at last succeeded in constructing a

monster plane capable of flying the Atlantic and back with a bomb load. As fast as these B-29s came into production they were shipped to the East, and at the bases in South China a formation was built up. On June 15, 1944, the bombers took off for the first time on a combat mission, flying to the great steel mills at Yawata in southern Japan. They bombed the mills and made the return journey without loss. Repeated raids followed; the new machine had a revolutionary fire-control system, and Japanese fighters found themselves unable to cope with the big bombers.

The reaction of the enemy was immediate and somewhat unexpected. Instead of seeking new means for dealing with the big planes in the air, they opened an offensive along the ground in southern China designed to cut the bases from under them. Since the beginning of the American war the Japanese had treated China more as a training area than as an actual theater, sending the new conscripts thither for a campaign which gained a few miles each year but accomplished little for the old imperial ambition of setting up a rail-and-road line from the productive areas in the south to ports at Shanghai and in Korea from which it would be a short voyage, through easily protected waters, to Japan.

The depredations of American submarines had now made such a road imperative if the Japanese

wished to keep their war machine going. The attacks of the B-29s merely furnished an additional reason. The Japanese threw heavy forces into the area and, in a confused campaign that washed up to the borders of the province of which Chungking is the center, won all the American air bases by the end of the summer.

CHAPTER XII

THE IMPERIAL DEFENSE-LINE COLLAPSES

By the late spring of 1944 the outer protective
screen of the Japanese empire had been thrown
down. The capture of Kwajalein and Eniwetok in
the Central Pacific and the steady advance of General MacArthur's forces along the shores of New
Guinea in the south had isolated among the islands
so many of the enemy's best troops that the make-
up of his army was seriously affected. His great
bases at Truk and Rabaul were converted into useless appendages which would only become func-
tional again if he regained control of the sea. Even
so, it was impossible for the Allies to drive home
an attack against either Japan or the stolen Indies.
Beginning with Japan itself, a great semicircle of
islands sweeps down below the equator, each within
easy flying distance of the next, all strongly fortified
and provided with fields for the planes on which
the Japanese were now placing great reliance.

From this protective chain the heart of the empire was distant by a mileage almost equal to the

width of the Atlantic. Some point in this circle must be seized and set up as an American base before the true attack could begin. The most centrally located and therefore the most strategically desirable of these island points were those of the Marianas group—Guam, Saipan, and Tinian—whose seizure would cut the main line of enemy communications southward and whose possession would furnish new fields for the B-29s, in addition to the advantages they had as harbors. As soon as Eniwetok had been secured, therefore, and reserves of material accumulated, it was decided to strike for the Marianas, a strategic concept which seems to owe much to the bold mind and long-range view of Fleet Admiral Ernest King.

The over-all commander for the Marianas operation was Admiral Raymond Spruance. His Fifth Fleet was divided into the fast carrier task force of Vice-Admiral Marc A. Mitscher and the battleship force of Vice-Admiral Lee. They were to furnish preliminary bombardments and cover against any operations of the Japanese navy, which was expected to emerge from its retirement for the defense of so vital an area. Close support of the landings was to be provided by a squadron of old battleships under Rear-Admiral J. L. Oldendorf and by groups of escort carriers, here used for the first time in major combat operations. The landing force was two divisions of Marines and one of army

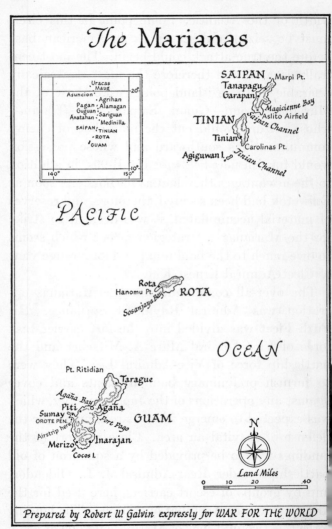

The Marianas

Uracas
Maug
Asuncion
Pagan · Agrihan
Guguan · Alamagan
Anatahan · Sariguan
· Medinilla
SAIPAN · TINIAN
· ROTA
· GUAM

SAIPAN   Marpi Pt.
Tanapagu
Garapan
Magicienne Bay
TINIAN   Saipan Channel   Aslito Airfield
Tinian
Carolinas Pt.
Agiguwan I.   Tinian Channel

PACIFIC

Rota
Hanomu Pt.   ROTA
Sosanjaya Bay

OCEAN

Pt. Ritidian
Tarague
Agaña Bay
Piti   Agana
Sumay   Port Pago   GUAM
OROTE PEN.
Airstrip here
Merizo   Inarajan
Cocos I.

N

Land Miles
0   10   20   40

Prepared by Robert W. Galvin expressly for WAR FOR THE WORLD

troops (27th), all under command of Marine Major-General Holland Smith.

The attack was set for middle June and a number of subsidiary operations were undertaken to conceal to the last moment the precise point of impact—bombing raids by B-24s from the Aleutians, the first attacks of the B-29s on the Japanese homeland, and a series of long-range raids from bases in the MacArthur area against such points as Truk and Palau in the Carolines. The initial landing was to be made on Saipan. The general plan was for Mitscher's fast carriers to fly strikes from some distance out on June 12 to destroy the local Japanese air defenses and to begin the attack against defenses aground. The fast battleships would follow with a gunnery attack. It was expected that the first Japanese reaction would be to stage down quantities of relief air groups through the Bonins. Mitscher would divide his forces after the first attack, sending two of his fast carrier groups north to strike at the Japanese among these islands. Meanwhile the escort carriers and slow battleships would arrive off Saipan with the landing forces, and these more deliberate units would provide support and cover for the invasion, while Mitscher's carriers and Lee's battleships were left free to deal with any move by the Japanese fleet.

The enemy scout planes managed to work through Mitscher's patrols and caught sight of his

armada a day early. As a result he speeded up his attack, striking the Marianas fields on June 11 instead of the 12th and repeating the attack the following day with gunnery help from the battleships. By afternoon of this second day the local Japanese air groups in the Marianas had been disposed of with little loss to ourselves. On the 13th the escort carriers arrived with Oldendorf's battleships and Vice-Admiral J. J. Clark was detached for the run up to the Bonins. He arrived on the 15th in weather so heavy there was some doubt whether planes could be flown at all. Nevertheless his strike groups got away and achieved surprise on the Japanese at Chichi Jima, Haha Jima, and Iwo Jima, where, exactly as expected, planes in considerable numbers were discovered on their way down to the Marianas and were very nearly wiped out in a two-day strike.

The Marines had meanwhile been flung on the beaches at the southwestern face of Saipan on both sides of the sugar-mill town of Charan Kanoa. The preliminary shelling and bombing was far heavier than at Kwajalein or Eniwetok, but Saipan is a large steep island of igneous rock. As soon as the advance to the beach began, it became clear that the Japanese had many guns still in action among the rocks and ravines.

Casualties at the southern of the two landing points were high, the concealed enemy guns firing with great accuracy at a line of reef and smashing

up both most of the amphibious tanks and the landing vessels loaded with artillery. The objective for
the day was not reached, but the two landings
joined up and when at daybreak of the second day
the Japanese tried a tank attack at the center it
was completely broken up by fire from the ships.
The Japanese began to retire to the steep slopes of
Mt. Tapotchau which furnishes the central backbone of the island, as the Marine force pivoted
on its left to drive them in that direction. But the
enemy had both greater forces and better positions
than anticipated. It was necessary to put in the
army division, which it had been hoped to hold
in reserve for the scheduled operation against
Guam. These troops were moved in behind the
Marines at the southern beachhead and thrust eastward toward the island's big airfield, Aslito. It was
slow work as the Japanese had many ingenious positions in caves with armored doors which opened
just long enough to let concealed guns fire. But by
the 19th the army men had gained control of the
airfield.

NOT since October, 1942, had the Japanese carrier
forces been in action. In the interval since that
time their naval air service had been completely
reconstructed—new pilots trained, new carriers in
service. Now in June, 1944, they had available five
large carriers (three of them larger than any of

ours) and four of the lighter type. The staff had
worked out an ingenious plan for their employment
in the defense of the Marianas. Powerful air
groups, at least equal to the strength of three or
four carriers more, would be staged down through
the Bonins to fall on our ships, which must neces-
sarily stay near the landing points to furnish cover
for the troops. At the same time the enemy fleet
would leave its haunts in the Carolines and Philippines, run north to a point in the Philippine Sea
about 700 miles from the Marianas, and there fly
off its planes. Seven hundred miles is double the
range of a carrier plane and the Japanese carriers
would turn away as soon as these planes were
launched, thus preventing any counterattack by
the American carrier aircraft which had dealt so
severely with them before. But the Japanese dive
bombers and torpedo planes would inevitably find
our fleet so close to the Marianas that, after having
struck our ships a blow, the planes could land there
and then repeat the attack from fields in the
islands.

One part of this plan miscarried when Admiral
Spruance anticipated it and sent Clark's carrier
north to break up the Japanese air groups among
the Bonins. But in exchange for this the enemy
had a most encouraging report from its commander
on Saipan, Admiral Nagumo, that he had sunk
at least one American battleship, damaged several

carriers and other vessels, and that the beachhead was only weakly held. Part of this was the result of a fake landing attempt meant to be "repulsed"; the rest can be accounted for only by the Japanese system of politeness, which did not allow commanders to report to the Emperor anything less than success.

The Japanese had, however, suffered another disaster of which they were still ignorant. As their fleets made north to the Carolines they had been spotted by American submarines as early as the 14th and had been reported to Admiral Spruance. The submarines continued to trail them. As the Japanese planes flew off on the morning of June 19, the submarine *Cavalla* closed in and put three torpedoes into the veteran large carrier *Shokaku,* and *Albacore* hit the new carrier *Taiho* with another torpedo. Far to the east that same morning the army troops had captured Aslito field. Admiral Spruance turned southwest, with his battleships between the carriers and the onrushing Japanese, and cleared his decks by sending all the dive bombers in to tear up Orote Point Field on Guam, the last one in the Marianas where enemy planes could land. His fighter patrols were all up, so numerous that they alone outnumbered all the machines that the Japanese had in the air. They encountered their enemies while the latter were still in cruising formation and at cruising level.

The Japanese attack thus became a complete failure; they secured but one bomb hit, on the armor of a battleship where it did little damage. Four hundred and two Japanese planes were shot down for the greatest loss to an air service of any single day in the war, and even the planes that escaped crashed on landing. The Japanese naval air service, so carefully rebuilt, had been destroyed with a single blow.

Admiral Spruance hung in the offing until nearly twilight, uncertain whether there might not be more Japanese planes behind these. When it developed that there were not, he speeded up on the trail of the enemy fleet, now making for the shelter of the Ryukyus. The next day, June 20, he pursued all day, confident that he could overtake them if they were following their usual practice of trying to get the damaged carrier home. Late in the afternoon they were found at the very limit of airplane range from our carriers, and though, if sent out, strike groups could not return to our ships till after dark, Spruance flew them off.

They reached the Japanese fleet about 6:00 P.M. in fading light and found it well scattered, with almost no fighter protection and running fast. Our own planes had also became somewhat scattered during the search and the attack lacked the coördination of some that had been delivered earlier in the war, but it was deadly enough. All the big

Japanese carriers were hit and two of the light ones —one of the latter so heavily that although she was dragged home she never again put to sea. *Shokaku* had gone down as a result of the submarine *Cavalla's* torpedoes; the *Taiho,* largest carrier in the enemy service, had blown up; the big *Hitaka* sank as the result of air attacks and her sister *Hayataka* was taken home in such condition that she too was out of the war. A destroyer was sunk and two of the fast tankers upon which the Japanese fleet depended for long-range mobility.

Our forces paid for their victory with 47 planes, mostly lost in crash or water landings in the dark when they had returned to their carriers with their last drops of fuel. Many of the aviators were saved when Admiral Mitscher, though deep in enemy waters, took the bold step of flinging the fleet's searchlight beams aloft as homing beacons.

WHILE the American fleet was taking in its planes far to the west on that evening of June 20, 1944, a minor air attack had come upon the ships grouped off Saipan and smashed one of them. The planes could clearly have come from nowhere but down the line of the Bonins, and to Admirals Spruance and Mitscher it seemed that this might be the beginning of a new effort in force. Admiral Clark with his carrier groups was rushed back to Iwo Jima. The diagnosis proved correct; he found the

place swarming with Japanese planes and fought a severe air battle with them on the 22nd. Like some of the formations encountered among the Solomons, these Japanese seemed to have been poorly or hastily trained. They lost 60 planes against only two of ours, and, after more of them had been destroyed on the ground in a second attack, the remainder turned back to Japan.

On shore the 4th Marine Division had worked right across the island to its eastern beaches and had turned north. The army division, leaving some formations behind to clear out the caves, moved into the center of the line around Mt. Tapotchau. They were slow in the movement and slow in attacking after it. The Japanese managed to reorganize around their central position and push infiltration attacks into the flanks of the two Marine divisions. Because of this, a famous controversy later developed: army leaders claimed that their more deliberate method of procedure saved lives; the Marines insisted that their rapid smashing attacks broke the back of resistance early and made mopping up largely a matter of careful patrolling. The question is technical; but there seems to have been something wrong with the leadership of the army division, which made its attacks with poor coördination throughout. Finally, after the advance had worked slowly forward, against the type of opposition always given by the Japanese, till it

reached a point four miles from the tip of the island, the enemy counterattacked.

It was a suicide charge, which might have been expected, but it broke through the 27th, wiping out one of its battalions, and got in among the Marine artillery positions. Many of the 15,000 casualties in the land fighting on Saipan occurred on this occasion, and the commander of the army division was removed. The Japanese dead on the island numbered over 28,000; many more were sealed in caves, never to be counted, some of them not being disposed of till six months after July 10, when the conquest of the island was declared complete.

The necessity of beating off the Japanese fleet and the prolonged resistance on Saipan had thrown the attack on Guam out of schedule, as also that against the small island of Tinian, which is within artillery range of southern Saipan. The double task was undertaken on July 21, that is, as soon as new troop formations could be staged from the United States and Hawaii through the Marshalls. The 3rd Marine Division, a Marine provisional brigade almost a division strong, and the 77th Army Division were involved.

There was no Japanese opposition by sea this time and the enemy air forces had been driven off, so the harassments and distractions were far less. Nevertheless the campaign itself showed that the

lessons of Saipan had been well learned. Ships and planes kept up such close and constant support that organized resistance was broken by August 10, without any formal battles. Seven thousand of the 17,000 Japanese killed on the island were not eliminated till after this date. The fanaticism of the resistance is indicated by the fact that the prisoners numbered only 483.

As soon as the islands were secured, great numbers of both army and navy construction workers were moved in, the latter to set up naval base installations for the move forward against the heart of the Japanese empire, the former to provide the long landing fields and elaborate shop installations necessary to support a large force of B-29 bombers. The battles in the Marianas had given us the gateway to Japan and a centralized assembly point from which any place around the great circuit of the empire could be attacked. They had also resulted in the virtual destruction of the most powerful arm of the Japanese fleet—though this was not realized at the time, since it was not known how heavy the damage had been to the enemy carriers in the great action of June 19–20, a victory fully as decisive as Midway.

CHAPTER XIII

THE GREAT INVASION

THE assault on what Hitler called "The Fortress of Europe" was primarily a logistic operation, a question of getting adequate supplies ashore to enable our troops to maintain themselves once they had landed, and of keeping up from the rear a flow of food, ammunition, and equipment. The Germans had systematically stripped the districts along the coast; the experience of Italy showed that their destruction of everything that would serve an army was so thorough that the attacking forces might almost as well be pitched into a jungle. Until the supply problem was solved, tactical and strategic questions could not even be considered.

The Germans were known to have made the problem as difficult as possible by heavily fortifying and garrisoning all the ports along the coast of Europe with quay capacity sufficient to support an army. The ports themselves were heavily mined and had immense numbers of guns of all calibres so mounted as to bear both out to sea and inward toward the land approaches; smaller pieces sup-

plied interlocking belts of fire to cover the forts
from infantry infiltration. The artillery positions
were usually dug into hill slopes or heavily covered
with concrete as a protection against air attack;
many of the guns were those removed from the
Maginot Line.

Between the ports, at all the beaches where landings might reasonably be expected, an immense
amount of work had been done by laborers impressed from eastern Europe. Underwater obstacles, mainly of steel, had been deeply planted and
linked together to tear the bottoms out of landing
craft. Many beaches were mined in addition. In
general, the strands of France are backed at a little
distance by a line of bluffs; here artillery of all
calibres had been mounted, the foreshore and all
the open country behind the bluffs had been
studded with tank traps, and practically all the
small cottages so common in this part of France
had been evacuated of their inhabitants and converted into pillboxes. In all these installations
there were permanent garrison troops, under orders to know the country thoroughly.

The German system of defense, of course, had
the disadvantage of locking up many troops, some
of their best, in fortresses at the very perimeter of
the territory to be defended, and leaving the Ger
man area commanders weak in mobile reserves for
counterattacking once a landing had been effected

It was a handicap they felt constrained to accept, not only because the Allied strength in aviation and vehicles made a war of movement peculiarly favorable to our side but also because the spring of 1944 brought American heavy bomber formations to Europe in such vastly increased numbers that 1,000-plane raids became common and there were some that doubled this figure.

The characteristic feature of the air war in the winter and spring of 1944 was a shift in emphasis on the part of the attack to the Luftwaffe, which was assailed both directly in the skies and at its fields, and indirectly at its factories. By May a diminution in the German fighter strength was encountered. This was not because there was a pronounced falling off in numbers of the German fighters but because of the comparative decrease in numbers through the enormous growth of the U.S. Eighth Air Force, which had by this time come to outnumber the home-based British. Bombing had not succeeded in wiping out German factories; by dispersing and digging in they managed to stay in production. But the damage caused was so serious—especially in places like the great railroad hub of Berlin, more than three quarters of which was burned out in a series of raids during March— that it was clear to the Nazi High Command that so formidable a force of bombers could make military movements around the area of a landing more

than a little uncertain. This furnished them with an additional reason for basing their defense on clinging to the seaports, with delaying defense elsewhere and counterattack against the Allied means of communication.

This was known to be the German method and it dictated Allied strategy. Our forces must contemplate taking a major army into Europe across open beachheads and supporting them in the same manner perhaps throughout an entire campaign, for there was no guarantee that a port could be won at an early date or that it would be any more useful than Naples after it had been gained. In turn, this had much to do with the choice of the spot for the invasion. It had to be an area which the larger type of landing craft could reach directly from England without the necessity of loading and unloading from transports. It had to be one from which troops could operate under the constant protection of Allied air power until they had won ground enough to provide their own strips; it should be a place near a good harbor and where the German communications were subject to bombing attack.

These conditions were met by the Cotentin Peninsula of Normandy, and it was upon this peninsula that the choice fell—a major factor being that the German communications ran back across the deep and wide Seine River and that there were numerous

bottlenecks at the bridges. Thinking we might strike there, the Germans deployed one army group with reserves and armor to meet the attack. But precisely because of the communications question they considered it quite as probable that the attack would come in the region of Calais, which was not only far nearer the English coast but had the added advantage that our advance could be made without supply lines stretching back across the Seine and Somme. The adjacent ports were also more numerous and better. The Germans accordingly deployed their second and larger army group in the Calais area.

For the solution of the fundamental problem of ports the Allies conceived the device of two completely artificial harbors, with breakwaters partly constructed of worn-out ships but mainly of huge caissons set up in England. The question of landing craft admitted of no solution through ingenuity; neither did that of supplies. The second, indeed, caused so much difficulty and involved so many executive decisions that for many months it occupied nearly all the time of General Eisenhower and his staff to the exclusion of more purely military problems. On more than one occasion the suggestion was made by those highest in governmental and military circles that the whole invasion plan be postponed or limited in scope.

Mr. Churchill in particular entered continual ob-

jections; he had always wished to invade Europe
from the south, and though at the historic Quebec
conference of May, 1943, his arguments had been
overborne and the decision taken, he always found
new questions to raise. Not the least of General
Eisenhower's titles to fame is that he insisted on
pushing "Operation Overlord" (as it was called)
through as planned and that he managed to see a
way through each objection from below and interference from political sources as these came up. He
insisted that the whole fate of the war depended
upon this invasion; that a failure or a partial success would return the initiative to the Germans as
their own failure in Egypt and partial success in
Russia had transferred it to the Allies. Again and
again officers of the highest rank and greatest
ability approached the General with suggestions
that the plan for aviation support would not work
—that the underwater obstacles would prove fatal
—that the invasion ought to be cut to three divisions in the initial stages—and particularly that the
plan of landing three airborne divisions would produce casualties up to 70 or 80 percent. To all he
replied, "I will take the responsibility," and insisted
that the plan of the Quebec conference be carried
through as made.

The question of landing craft, however, was one
he could not solve alone. They must be used in vast
numbers to make the initial wave of assault very

strong, so that the beachheads could be rapidly extended to a distance that would make it impossible for the Germans to interrupt the flow of supplies and reinforcements by gunfire. The Sicilian landing had succeeded rapidly because this was achieved; the landings at Salerno and Anzio had been strategic failures because it was not achieved. The shipyards, now relieved of some of the pressure for antisubmarine vessels, broke all records in supplying landing craft, but by March it was already evident that they could not meet the requirements for the invasion to begin in May, as originally planned. The date was shoved back to early June, though this placed it at the edge of a dangerous season for winds and tides. The invasion of south France, which was scheduled to take place simultaneously, was moved along to a time when the landing craft which had been used in Normandy could be shipped thither for the second invasion.

THE attack on the continent of Europe began tactically toward the middle of March, 1944, with a double change in tactics by the Allied bombers. The damaged Luftwaffe was still capable of mounting powerful local operations, and neither the bombing of factories nor the burning out of whole cities was bringing it down as rapidly as desired. On the other hand, the Mediterranean Air Force had badly damaged the Rumanian refineries and there was

evidence that German ground transport on the long Russian front was beginning to suffer from a short-age of gasoline. Long-range bombers, both British and American, were concentrated against German synthetic oil plants, installations which it was im-possible either to conceal or to place underground. Other targets were attacked, of course, but only as diversions or when, for some reason, a formation could not reach its primary objective.

At the same time the short-range bombers were fanned out all across northern France in a series of raids against communicaions, particularly rail-roads and bridges. These raids were on the whole very effective. By the date of the invasion the Ger-man transportation system in northern France was in such a state of disorganization that, if the area were not actually isolated, major military move-ments could only be made slowly. On the night of June 5 a thousand British heavy bombers suddenly attacked the whole Normandy coast. At daybreak the task was taken over by as many American planes, and under lowering skies of the following dawn the invasion was launched.

To furnish gunnery cover, six battleships stood in offshore, accompanied by a host of lighter ves-sels both British and American. A good many of the latter were lost, more from mines than from the shore batteries with which the German Com-mander, Rommel, hoped to make the invasion

failure while it was still on the water. The general
Allied plan of operation was designed to break
down precisely such a defense, with both ships and
planes assigned in great numbers to attack targets
on call from troop leaders at the beach. Four thousand boats of various sizes were employed in the
landing; not even from a plane could all be seen
at once, so far did the armada stretch across the
horizon.

The tactical plan called for the British Second
Army (Montgomery) to land at the mouth of the
Orne River, advance as quickly as possible to the
line Bayeux-Caen, and there form a fighting defensive flank. An airborne division preceded them
to the region of Caen, and other airborne troops
were dropped as far away as Havre and Rouen to
interrupt enemy communications and to conceal
the true point of the main effort.

The beach landing in this area was successful
against comparatively light opposition and the airborne men gained possession of bridges across the
Orne north of Caen, but the aerial effort south of
that town failed, and during the four days following the invasion Rommel put an armored division
through Caen which drove the British from their
partial possession of the town and from most of
the Orne bridges. But at the same time the Second
ined its beachheads, captured Bayeux, and over-
n an area seven miles deep, while Rommel's ar-

The Cotentin Peninsula

Bournemouth
Southampton
Portsmouth
Brighton

ISLE OF WIGHT

N

Land Miles
0   10   20   40

BR. SECOND ARMY
U.S. FIRST ARMY

6 June, 1944

Auderville
Cherbourg
Barfleur
St.Vaast
UTAH
OMAHA
GOLD
JUNO
SWORD
Le Havre
Carteret
Grandcamp
Honfleur
La Haye
Isigny
Courseulles
Trouville
Carentan
Bayeux
Ouistreham
Cabourg
Coutances
St. Lô
Caen
Granville

St. Malo
Avranches
Dol
Pontorson

ENGLAND
Southampton
Portsmouth
Plymouth
Channel
English
Cherbourg
La Havre
COTENTIN PENINSULA
NORMANDY
PARIS
BRITTANY
FRANCE

Prepared by Robert W. Galvin expressly for WAR FOR THE WORLD

mored attack was broken up by guns from the sea.

Further west the main effort was made by American troops under the command of General Bradley, along a front aggregating some thirty miles, the over-all design being to break through across the Cotentin Peninsula and to isolate the port of Cherbourg for attack from the rear. As soon as Cherbourg fell, major forces were to be poured in for a drive into Brittany. Two airborne divisions preceded the landing to gain communication points. There were two beachheads; Utah Beach on the west and Omaha Beach. At Utah Beach, Major General Collins's VII Corps broke through light resistance early, crossed a belt of marshes, and hooked up with the 82nd Airborne Division to capture the important road junction of Carentan, half cutting German communications with Cherbourg. This was accomplished by June 10.

The most difficult situation was encountered by Major General Gerow's V Corps (1st and 29th Divisions) at Omaha Beach, between Utah Beach and the British landing. The mines and underwater obstacles had not been effectively cleared either by demolition squads or fire. They wrecked many of the landing craft, and the advance elements of engineer troops found themselves so pinned down by fire that they could not accomplish their task of breaching the barbed wire and the system of

antivehicle obstacles. The fire came from guns mounted in a series of low sandy bluffs that looked down onto the beach from a few hundred yards back. There was so much earth and concrete over these guns that they were immune to air attack and they were so well armored as to be impervious to destroyer fire. The battleships had to be summoned with their powerful artillery and while they were firing, elements of the 1st and 29th were heavily counterattacked by a German infantry division which, by the purest chance, had been conducting anti-invasion maneuvers at just this point

Throughout June 6 and most of the 7th the struggle at Omaha Beach was close and doubtful and the casualties heavy, but the 2nd Division poured through the remnants of the two leader and, attacking southwest, won a communication point which isolated the German front line. The Germans were holding in natural positions formed by hedgerows of ancient growth, so tangled and with ditches so deep as to halt tanks, but their defense was parceled out and local because of the difficulty of moving troops. The counterattack by air failed completely.

By June 12 the beachhead lines were growing enough dry ground had been won near Carenta for the Allies to begin setting up landing strip The British were twenty miles in, we had 16 divisions on the shore, and the VII Corps had esta

lished a mass of maneuver on its own right flank. American casualties in getting the beachheads established were slightly over 7,300.

In the second phase of the invasion the British attacked Caen while General Collins's mass of maneuver, headed by the 82nd and the veteran 9th Division, struck straight across the Cotentin Peninsula, reaching the west coast on June 18. Thanks to the pinning effect of the British attack and their own troubles in moving troops, the Germans had now lost communication with Cherbourg. But on that same day, the 18th, came a check when one of the worst gales in the whole history of the English Channel blew up; it was to last four days.

The work of putting the artificial ports in position had begun as soon as our forces pushed far enough inland to eliminate the danger of German artillery, and it was now in full swing. The storm completely wrecked the port behind the American area at Omaha Beach, piling the shore so high with debris that engineering equipment destined for the front had to be diverted to the task of merely making a clearing. The British port at Arromanches was severely damaged and the caissons salvaged from Omaha had to be used to repair it. Instead of two artificial ports the invasion was now supported by only one, and that one long delayed. The shortage of equipment was felt at

once, particularly in such items as tanks and shop equipment, not very susceptible of being brought in across open beaches.

Moreover, the lowering skies of the storm almost completely blacked out the Allied infantry coöperation plans. Now for various reasons our command had decided to use planes for counterbattery work, long-range fire, and for other missions usually assigned to heavy artillery. Our troops were thus suddenly without this form of support while the Germans did have heavy artillery and their service was already superior in light pieces and mortars. The result was that for the time being they had fire superiority. Allied armor could hardly move; repeated infantry attacks by the British failed, and the south face of the front across the Cotentin Peninsula stabilized in a type of warfare resembling that of World War I.

On the northern front toward Cherbourg, German strength had been badly broken in the rush across the peninsula, and when General Collins put three divisions into the attack the enemy retreated to the area of his fortified port. By June 2 the siege began. The place was protected on the landward side by a series of hills, the whole interiors of which had been dug out and heavy guns mounted on several stories. These positions had to be assaulted by infantry advancing inch by inch under cover of constant shelling and bombing.

thousand heavy bombers were used in the attack on the 22nd. The battleships lay off the port, firing almost continuously; and one of them, *Texas*, suffered considerable damage from German guns.

The enemy's defense was conducted with great tactical skill. At night they counterattacked constantly, and once they won back a big fort that had already been captured. But as Allied control of the air was absolute, the Americans were able to move at will, concentrating now in one direction, now another. After a week of savage street fighting Cherbourg fell on June 27. Demolitions had been so thorough, and the harbor had been so completely blocked by mines, concrete, and sunken ships, that it was August before the first cargoes could come through. American casualties had now run to 23,000; but in Cherbourg the German loss had been nearly that number in prisoners alone.

THE British meanwhile had again and again attacked in the Caen region, a slow, dull, dogged fight under heavy artillery barrages which gained a few feet a day. On July 9 they had most of the town. After Cherbourg fell, the full American force swung into line with them, two fresh corps were landed to complete the American First Army, and the same type of advance began all across the peninsula. There were no tactics except at the lowest level; it was a straight slugging advance whose ob-

jective was to gain room for the employment of our troops. Every field with its hedgerows was a separate fortress and had to be reduced by siege operations, very costly in lives.

But the Germans were so harried by our aviation behind the lines and their reserves were so ground down by the ceaseless pressure of the British that they could not assemble forces for any major counterattack. They were forced to use their armor in support of small piecemeal attacks of about a battalion strength aimed at blunting the point of each successive Allied penetration. Early in July the hedgerow defenses lost much of their validity when American forces began mounting bulldozer scoops on the front of heavily armored tanks and driving them right through. Their air forces gave the Germans no help; thanks to their transportation troubles, they were constantly embarrassed for lack of gasoline and sometimes of ammunition. Toward the end of June they lost Marshal Rommel their Supreme Commander, when he was mortally wounded by a bullet from an Allied plane that caught him on the road in his car.

His replacement was Marshal Rundstedt, one of the ablest of the German commanders, who had played a great part in the drive through France in 1940. Before he could develop a new strategy of his own, General Bradley's men, after two weeks of close and bloody fighting, captured the great

road and railroad center of St. Lô, hub of the whole peninsula. Rundstedt reported to Berlin that his situation had become dangerous. His reserves, especially in armor, were almost exhausted. He could get no reinforcements from the rear and was not being allowed to draw on the unemployed German army in the Calais area, since the German High Command knew that we still had forces in England and expected us to attempt the Calais region with another landing. Rundstedt's suggestion was that he retreat from the Normandy region and all central France, building up a new line of defense behind the Seine. He believed he could hold this position, with the aid of the Calais troops.

The fact that so able a German commander could report in favor of abandoning the campaign is the best indication of the success of the only invasion of the European Continent ever achieved from the sea. To people on the Allied side it seemed that the gains were small and achieved at great cost, and this was true if geography alone were considered. But the whole structure of the German defense had been shaken. The army was so short of reserves that Polish and Russian prisoners were pressed into service.

Rundstedt's report fell in the period that witnessed an officers' conspiracy against the life of Adolf Hitler. The German Führer considered the report treasonable, ordered the position to be held

at any cost, and removed Rundstedt. Thus at a critical juncture the enemy were driven to the discontinuity of strategy and method that follows such rapid changes in command, and the incoming leaders were forced to undertake a task they did not believe they could perform.

THE invasion had not taken place a moment too soon. On June 15, after the beachheads had been linked, observers in London saw a streak of flame down the sky and heard a heavy explosion. It looked like the crash of a German bomber and they cheered; but as three, four, and many others followed, they realized it could not be that and the cheering stopped. It was, in fact, the beginning of a new age in warfare.

The objects that had trailed across the sky were aerial torpedoes, each carrying about the same explosive charge as those used at sea and flying on a pair of short wings, pilotless, propelled by a jet or reaction motor which had a close affinity to the rocket. They had come from a series of carefully camouflaged ramps on the coast in the Calais area. Though their accuracy was low, the Germans had little difficulty in hitting a target so big as the city of London, against which most of the new weapons were aimed. Christened V-1 by the Germans and buzz-bombs by the Allies, the bombs flew very high and at a speed of over 400 miles an hour, s

that only a very few fighter planes stood any
chance of shooting them down. When their fuel
was exhausted they nosed down at a sharp angle
to explode.

The casualties they caused were considerable.
By the end of July, 4,735 people had been killed
in London and over 14,000 wounded. The material
damage was far beyond that caused by the heaviest
air raid—so serious was it, in fact, that in the
opinion of many soldiers the invasion of France
could not have been launched at all if the buzz-
bomb attack had begun a few weeks earlier. Even
as it was, it caused serious diversions of men and
material from the attack on Europe. Barrage bal-
loons around London were increased to over 2,000
in number. Over 1,350 anti-aircraft guns were
brought down to the coast and established in batteries in an effort to catch the attacking robots before they could make their way inland. Many air
squadrons and radar stations were told off to similar duties, while numerous planes were employed
in bombing the launching sites.

They had been bombed before; in fact, the British had been aware that something of the sort was
coming ever since the fall of 1943. In November
of that year the Germans had already built over
a hundred launching sites along the coast, every
one of which was bombed out so that the work had
to be begun again in the following spring. In fact,

the defense and counteroffense kept fairly well ahead of the V-1 attacks. Of more than 8,000 of the weapons launched only 2,300 reached their objective. Moreover, the Nazis spent so much time and productive capacity on them that their air service suffered severely. The attacks also had a strategic effect unfavorable to the Germans by helping to persuade them to detain in the Calais area the troops that might have been much better employed in Normandy.

CHAPTER XIV

FRANCE SET FREE

THE importance to an army of having a road-hub close behind its lines like that at St. Lô is that troops coming to it from a variety of directions may be fanned out along the radii of a circle, while the defenders must take the long way round the circumference. This was especially true in Normandy where the hedgerows and dense undergrowth made military traffic impossible except along the roads. When the American 29th Division captured St. Lô on July 18, 1944, after two weeks of desperate house-to-house fighting, and pushed the Germans two miles beyond, General Eisenhower was in a peculiarly good position for a major offensive against the left flank of the enemy line across the Cotentin Peninsula. That line swept in a curve around our front with its flank resting on the sea north of Coutances, and many of its supporting roads were under fire.

The strategic situation also was favorable. The German command had just changed for the second time within a month and some of the new staff

officers were none too familiar with their duties. The violent attacks of the British Second Army and the Canadian First had unsettled their lateral communications at the root northeast of Caen. Reinforcements for the western end of the line had to go by a considerable circuit. To crown all, General George Patton, our best attack commander, had just landed through the beachhead ports with his Third Army, including no less than four armored divisions, a fact of which the Germans were still ignorant.

On July 25 General Eisenhower opened his offensive on a bright, sunny morning with a terrific bombardment from 1,575 heavy bombers, followed instantly by the same number of lighter planes. (An unfortunate feature of this attack was the death of Lieutenant General Lesley J. McNair, commander of the American ground forces, through an accidental bomb hit.) Great gaps were blasted in the hedgerows; through them poured four infantry divisions, headed toward Coutances on the coast against the opposition of only two German divisions. The bulk of the enemy strength was concentrated farther to the east against what they regarded as the very dangerous Canadian-British offensive. On the first day our troops gained two miles and cut one of the few lateral highways remaining to the enemy.

On the second day four entire divisions of tanks

the first arrivals of the Third Army, rushed through the gap thus created. By July 28 the 4th Armored Division was in Coutances, from which point it turned southeast, hooking up with other armored formations and infantry to the east. The whole front now began to swing with St. Lô as a hinge. Many Germans were cut off and captured along the coast, as were many more in the area of the great break-through. Our forces found the enemy rear areas in a state of disorganization and captured whole companies that had not been able to obtain orders from their own headquarters. The First Army swung eastward against this door of the German left flank; the Third, General Patton in person up with the advance, fanned its 2nd, 3rd, 4th, and 6th Armored Divisions out to the coast at a dozen points.

On July 30 the 3rd Armored Division reached Avranches. This is an old walled town of 8,000 population, of considerable importance because its position at the head of a shallow estuary backed by rough country allows it to control access to all western Normandy. The few German troops in the place were able to hold it that day against the American vanguards, but by the next morning our infantry arrived and the town fell. That same day General Eisenhower reorganized his High Command, giving the First Army to Lieutenant General Courtney H. Hodges and making General

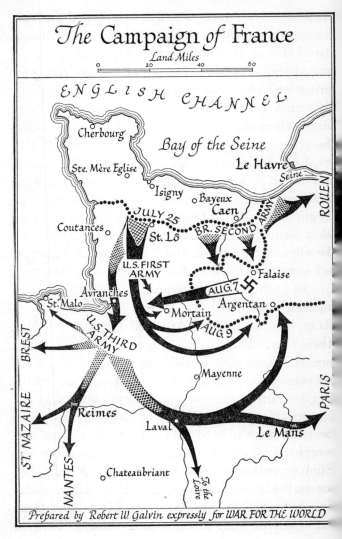

The Campaign of France

Land Miles

0   20   40   60

ENGLISH CHANNEL

Cherbourg

Bay of the Seine

Le Havre

Seine

Ste. Mère Eglise

ROUEN

Isigny

Bayeux

Caen

JULY 25

BR. SECOND ARMY

Coutances

St. Lô

U.S. FIRST ARMY

Falaise

AUG.7

Avranches

Argentan

St. Malo

Mortain

BREST

U.S. THIRD ARMY

AUG. 9

ST. NAZAIRE

Mayenne

PARIS

Reimes

Laval

Le Mans

NANTES

Chateaubriant

To the Loire

Prepared by Robert W. Galvin expressly for WAR FOR THE WORLD

Bradley commander of an army group including both this force and General Patton's. Up to this time Montgomery had been theoretically in tactical charge of ground forces, though in a practical sense he had confined most of his attention to the British-Canadian portion of the front. His work in pinning down major German forces in that area had been excellent and had made possible the St. Lô break-through, but General Eisenhower was somewhat dissatisfied with his slowness in maneuver and, for the open-country operations now beginning, wished to draw on the enormous tactical skill and ability to make snap decisions of Omar Bradley, who had continually kept the Germans off balance on his front.

The Germans had withdrawn formations piecemeal in an attempt to save their crumbling left flank, where Hodges's attack threatened to roll up their whole line. Now, as the seriousness of the break-through fully justified Rundstedt's apprehensions and they realized that Patton was already in France, major forces were brought down from the Calais area. The six armored divisions that had been holding the position around Caen were shifted westward in a quick effort to break through the First Army's front toward Avranches. Fortunately for us, the German withdrawals weakened the Caen line before the troops from Calais could fill the gap. The Canadians and British attacked south-

ward and got across the lateral road to Avranches on July 31. The result was that the German counterattack lacked both surprise and force. It made some gains and for a time cut the corridor between their left flank and the sea to some twelve miles. But the American First Army held firm, and through that 12-mile corridor General Patton continued to pour the Third Army in an endless stream of tanks and truck-borne infantry.

By August 2 the 6th Armored was in Pontorson and the 2nd Armored well along the Brittany coast road at St. Malo. A compilation that day showed that a week of continuous battles had given us 19,000 German prisoners; four more divisions of enemy troops escaped only by rapid retreat into Brittany. The very speed of the break-through, indeed, militated against attaining one of the objectives in this direction. It had been hoped to gain one of the great ports, Brest or Lorient, but the Germans did not have time to move troops out of these and when the armored columns of Patton's men rolled up on August 7 they found the enemy still strongly established in both places.

THE Breton ports had, however, become secondary objectives by August 7, 1944, at which date the entire province, except those ports, was cleared of Germans and it was plain that General Hodges' men would be able to hold the heavy and persisten

efforts to break through and cut off the Avranches corridor. By this date the dogged advance of the Canadians had broken through within only five miles of Falaise and a dazzling prospect opened up.

The bulk of the Nazi strength was now well to the north and west, between Vire and Mortain. Thanks to the operations of the Canadians the only highways the Germans had for supply or retreat ran in a southeasterly direction through Falaise and Argentan, thence back across the Seine as far east as Rouen and Paris. A large proportion of the Germans were slow foot-marching infantry with horse transport; and Patton was on the loose southward with strong formations of armor and mechanized infantry. If he could be swung north and east, major portions of that German army might be cut off; and while the effort would demand the utmost from men and machines, it was worth trying with such a driver as Patton behind it.

Bradley made another of his famous tactical snap decisions, and orders were issued to try the maneuver. Infantry and men of the French underground (*Maquis*) were sent to blockade the Breton ports, and the armor came streaming out of that province as rapidly as it had moved in. Other detachments ran south to hold the main bridges across the Loire against the rather unlikely possibility that the Germans in southern France would be able to organize a counterattack against Pat-

ton's new rear, as his main force hurried north with
its weight on the right wing toward Le Mans. That
town was assaulted on August 9 and taken from
weak German formations; next day Alençon fell.
Patton fanned mechanized troops out along the
roads to Paris (they moved so rapidly that some
had to be supplied by air) with directions to turn
west toward Rouen, but the bulk of his strength
was driven on Argentan.

The Canadians attacked south toward Falaise,
the British east toward the mouth of the Seine.
A special air force order called for every airplane
fit for flight to be operated constantly against the
Seine bridges and Germans in motion. The action,
known as the battle of the Falaise Pocket, lasted
until August 16. It was fought chiefly in rain,
with the fiercest kind of fighting, day and night
against Germans who had now fully realized their
danger and who had planted extensive mine fields
and brought up all the artillery they could muster
to hold up the narrowing escape gap between Patton and the Canadians. Neither Argentan nor Falaise was taken during the battle and in a technical
sense the German claim that their Seventh Army
(the unit involved) escaped has some justification
But it was true only in the most restricted technical sense, for never was an army in worse condition
than the German force whose remnants reached the
north bank of the Seine on August 24.

They had lost 130,000 men in prisoners alone, a number exceeding all the Allied casualties put together since the invasion of France. Our forces buried 20,000 of their dead and if the wounded, who were never counted, reached the normal figure for fighting of this character, they were five to one of the killed. The German Seventh had lost nearly all its armor, most of its artillery and transport, and many of its headquarters staffs. It had in fact not so much escaped as been destroyed, and if toward the end of the month the port of Brest was able to beat off an assault it was chiefly because so many more of the enemy formations were now locked up in it and out of the war.

THE German unit occupying southern France was the Nineteenth Army, a formation well below the fighting-power level of those on the Atlantic coast. In that area, rougher and less populated than the industrial north, the French underground was particularly strong and had attained a considerable degree of military organization. The leadership was of the most varied sort; its activities ranged all the way from concealment of Allied aviators to attacks on means of communication and the assassination of collaborators with the Germans. It remained an essentially guerrilla organization, since the arms that were brought in by plane and submarine could consist of nothing beyond ma-

chine guns, grenades, and explosive charges, and with these it was impossible to meet tanks or artillery. Yet the activity of the *Maquis* was greatly intensified after Normandy was invaded; it soon became so serious that more than half of the Nineteenth German Army was required merely to assure communications for the rest. The result was that the long southern coastline was held by only two divisions and part of a third, while most of the remaining Nineteenth Army formations were parceled out in small groups across the countryside, in the worst possible position should the coast be broken through.

The fact that the Allied landing was contemplated was no secret from the Germans, whose aerial reconnaissance had spotted the ships of the invasion fleet assembling in Corsican harbors. They deduced with approximate accuracy both the date and the place of impact. But by this time General Patton's whirlwind had already burst through the German lines at Avranches in the north; the German High Command was forced to disregard appeals from the Nineteenth Army for reinforcements and planes, and the attack fell upon opponents struggling with a deep sense of discouragement and insufficiency.

The blow was delivered by a new U.S. Seventh Army under the command of Lieutenant-General Alexander M. Patch (who had led the infantry on

Guadalcanal) and the First French Army of General De Lattre de Tassigny, the whole headed by Lieutenant-General Jacob L. Devers, who had shifted to the Mediterranean when Eisenhower returned to London. The point of impact was around Cannes and St. Raphael on the east face of the obtuse peninsula that juts into the Mediterranean between the mouths of the Rhone and the Italian border. The date was August 15, 1944; the battleships and cruisers that had covered the Normandy invasion were present for gunnery support with many French ships, and close-in air cover was provided by an assemblage of seven British and two American escort carriers, while heavy bombers came up from the fields of Corsica and Sardinia.

Before dawn on Invasion Day strong formations of parachutists descended in the valley of the Argens River, which reaches the sea at St. Raphael, to seize the pass by which the Rhone Valley is reached from the landing area. Other parachutists gained the pass by which the Germans might reinforce the area from north Italy, but the enemy attempted no such operation. Westward near Bornes in the great bay formed by the Hyères Islands, the French forces went ashore and with an armored division leading began pushing along the coast toward Toulon. On the eastern beaches the Americans struck, all veterans of the hard fighting in Italy. There was strong resistance only in

spots and those not numerous, for information provided by the French underground was so accurate
that every defense installation had been heavily hit
by shells and bombs in the preliminary stages. Indeed, the area of the American landing was found
to be held by only two regiments, composed of
Poles and Czechs who had been pressed into the
German service and who surrendered at the first opportunity. Many similar formations were rounded
up by the underground in the rear areas and by
the third day of the landing the Allied forces already had over 10,000 prisoners while their own
casualties numbered under 2,000.

The French forces pressed rapidly west, masking
Toulon and laying siege to Marseille, which fell
on August 23 and was found in the same state of
wreckage as other port towns captured from the
Germans. Toulon was both more defensible and
had stronger guns. It was not taken till August 26,
after a week of bitter street fighting, also by French
forces.

Meanwhile the American VI Corps of General
Truscott was rushing through all the gaps toward
the broad Rhone Valley, meeting almost no resistance, for in view of the situation further north the
Germans had decided to pull out, leaving detach
ments behind to complicate our supply problem by
holding the ports. The decision was made too late
and the movement, hampered by the underground

and by American aviation, which now had fields in France, was made too slowly. At Montelimar on August 25 General Truscott's men got across the path of an armored division and parts of two others. There was a battle; nearly all the 15,000 Germans were killed or captured and they were forced to abandon 800 tanks.

Patch's columns pushed ahead rapidly, throwing out one wing to connect with the Third Army in the region of Paris on September 15, while another swung around the tip of Swiss territory which juts into France and came up to the Belfort Gap that leads to the plains of Alsace. Their brief campaign had yielded 50,000 prisoners, and the Nineteenth German Army, like the Seventh, had been substantially destroyed.

FOR Germans the disorganization caused by the Allied victories was less serious than it might have been in other services. Under their system, commands and staffs as far down as the regimental level are purely temporary. When groups as large as a battalion held together they could readily be assembled into new major formations. But the over-all position of the Germans was now thoroughly bad. The failure to hold Patch placed the new left flank of their position along the Seine at the end of August, 1944, in double jeopardy. The core of their forces was made up of the Fifteenth

Army, more properly a group of armies, which had been largely in the Calais region; there were also fragments of the Seventh Army and of the First, which had been holding central France and the Biscay ports.

The main concentrations were along the Seine between Paris and Le Havre, with only the slenderest formations of garrison troops and hastily found reinforcements east of the French capital. On this flank our forces had the highly mobile Third Army of General Patton. He had brought his formations up to the Seine on both sides of the French city on August 22, but those to the north and west were pulled out to fall in behind the rest for a move to the eastward to get around the weak German flank. Our First Army took over west of Paris on August 25. General Eisenhower much gratified French susceptibilities by allowing their Second Armored Division to be the first group into the city where they had captured the German garrison, 10,000 strong.

Beyond Paris, Patton crossed the Seine with ease and lunged north toward Rheims and the Belgian border, resting his right flank in the highlands of the Meuse, which river was reached on August 31. By that date, British, Canadians, and the American First Army all had strong bridgeheads across the lower Seine and the German High Command had lost interest in fighting for the retention of

Flanders and the buzz-bomb bases. They threw
heavy garrisons into the coastal ports—Calais, Le
Havre, Dunkirk, Ostend, Boulogne—and retreated
as rapidly as possible, resisting only by means of
rear guards, mine fields and demolitions. The situation was now completely fluid, with troops moving
rapidly in all directions, but thanks to the superiority of our forces in vehicles and in the air, the
Allies had the superior mobility at all times save
when the enemy chose to achieve a delay by sac-
rificing portions of their forces.

Even this did not always work, since the Germans had to swing through a long parabola while
the advance could often take short cuts. The VII
Corps of the U.S. First Army, moving north from
the Aisne crossings, reached Mons by September 3
close on the heels of the retreating enemy. Air
scouts brought in the astonishing news that strong
German forces were approaching from the southwest in column on the roads. The corps faced
around and took position; the enemy were an entire Nazi corps of five divisions, but without air
cover and with few tanks. In a savage two-day
battle they were surrounded and virtually wiped
out; 22,000 prisoners were taken in this most important action of the whole advance.

By September 15, in a rush that has few historical parallels, the British and Canadians were up
the line of the Scheldt where it runs west to the

North Sea, and had taken Antwerp, which they found, rather surprisingly, neither destroyed nor defended. From here their line ran southeast to meet that held by the American forces, who had reached a tiny corner of German territory opposite Aachen. From Aachen our line ran south, generally just inside the borders of Luxembourg, to where the Meuse turns northeast for its plunge through the Eiffel Mountains, and from here on south along the Meuse till the mountains of Alsace were reached. The Third Army held some bridge-heads across the Meuse and the Seventh had gained possession of the Belfort Gap, but in general the position had stabilized, the advance had been halted.

There were several reasons for this. One was that the Germans brought in reinforcements from their general reserve while our forces had been subjected to the amount of straggling unavoidable in so rapid an advance. This process was aided by many small pockets of isolated Germans, which had to be mopped up by detachments that later had to be brought back to their parent units, with resulting complication of traffic problems.

The second reason was that the fall rains of northern Europe had begun, and the lowering skies had their usual effect on the Allied air forces. The Germans had a great deal of heavy artillery in the positions to which they had retreated. Our forces

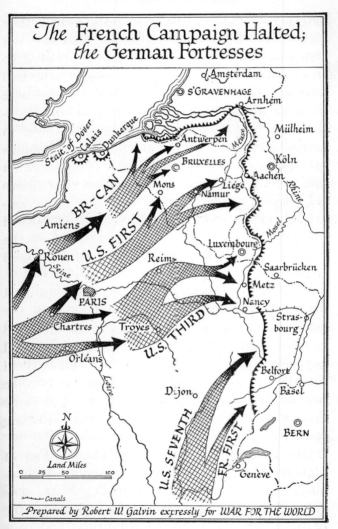

The French Campaign Halted; the German Fortresses

Prepared by Robert W. Galvin expressly for WAR FOR THE WORLD

had very few of these weapons, which can be moved forward slowly and with difficulty only, and the result was that the enemy's firepower was in general superior. Moreover, the positions now reached were so easily defensible that numbers counted for little and mobility for almost nothing. In the north the Nazis held the Scheldt, deep and wide, and the extensive system of islands at its mouth. They had opened the dikes and the ground was reduced to a quagmire, almost impassable for armor or mechanical vehicles.

South of this, down to the Meuse, our forces were up against the West Wall, or Siegfried Line, an extensive system of fortifications covering the whole frontier of Germany. It was not a solid line of forts but an interlocking belt of separate positions many miles deep, mostly underground and expertly camouflaged, heavily concreted and designed to resist all the forms of modern attack which the Germans themselves had brought into play in 1940. The Meuse is a deep stream with almost precipitous banks and runs through rough country where the avenues of traffic are few in number and sharply canalized. All along its eastern bank facing our troops were the fortifications of the old French Maginot Line; and this line was strengthened by modern installations at Thionville, Metz, and Nancy. South of this belt was the broken country of the Vosges, with more fortifications and poor

lines of communication on the Allied side, very good ones on the German.

But the main reason for the slowing up of the great drive was the question of supply. The abrupt halt of the Third Army, whose tanks had run half across France, is very striking. The Third had run short of both fuel and ammunition after reaching the Meuse, in spite of the fact that a pipeline had been built across the entire English Channel underwater and linked with a great express highway that had been constructed from Normandy to Paris to convey exactly these items up to the front. The French railroads had been systematically raided for rolling stock by the Germans during the occupation and systematically wrecked during the retreat. They could give little help. France had been plucked so clean that even much of the food for its civilian population had to be brought in—an enormous burden in addition to supplying the needs of the armies.

In dealing with this burden there was a serious bottleneck in port facilities. Cherbourg and the artificial harbor at Arromanches were long the only places through which ocean-going ships could be unloaded. Brest, indeed, fell to the attacks of the newly organized Ninth American Army under Lieutenant-General William H. Simpson on September 19; Boulogne was taken by the Canadians on September 18, following their capture of Le

Havre on the 12th. But the demolitions at Boulogne had been so thorough that it was considered impossible to repair the harbor in time to be of any use in this war. The capacity of Boulogne was small and it was the end of the year before Le Havre could be gotten into shape. Marseille, as soon as it was cleared, became a main reliance; 18,000 tons of supplies were moved through it daily, and ultimately 14 divisions of troops were landed there. But the use of Marseille involved a long journey by ships up through the Strait of Gibraltar at one end and a long journey by railroad at the other. The armies at the front continued to develop shortages.

Nevertheless General Eisenhower thought that by pressing the enemy before he had a chance to rally great results might be achieved. The method worked out was for the use of an airborne army under Lieutenant-General L. H. Brereton to turn the West Wall at its northern end. It had been intended to use this army, which consisted of two entire American airborne divisions and one British with a number of special groups, in operations in France, but the advance proved so rapid that an airborne movement was unnecessary. On September 17 the air army was launched in an attempt to gain crossings of the great rivers that flow west through Holland. Carried by nearly 3,000 planes, the 82nd and 101st American divisions were set

down near Eindhoven north of the Maas, to gain
the bridges. The British were dropped at Arnheim
north of the Waal mouth of the Rhine to win the
great bridge there. In support of this operation the
British Second Army attacked north toward the
Scheldt with the design of linking up to the airborne troops.

They had a cloudy day, which made German
anti-aircraft weak and ineffective. The two American divisions managed to organize their ground
and link up with the Second Army across the
Scheldt after several days of severe fighting. But
near Arnheim the Germans had two armored divisions in a rest area. As soon as the airborne British
landed they were assailed by overwhelming numbers of troops who had plenty of artillery and
armor while they had very little. All efforts at relief failed, and after a dogged defense the division
was nearly wiped out.

This event and the fact that our armies were
everywhere stalled in heavy fighting against strong
fortifications sent a wave of pessimism sweeping
through the country. While the Germans were
breaking across France, the Russians had been
making wide gains in the east and it seemed that
the Nazis could not hold out much longer. In fact
preparations for victory observances had been
made in many places. The Germans adroitly aided
his overconfidence by means of propaganda em-

phasizing their own despair and urging all citizens to take up arms, while exaggerating Allied gains by announcing that such places as Metz and Nancy had fallen after slight resistance. In addition, just at this juncture when the clearing of the Channel coast brought an end to the buzz-bomb attacks, the Germans appeared with the second and more terrible of their V-weapons, V-2, a true rocket which moved in the region of the stratosphere at such speed that no interception was possible. It could be fired from North Holland and even from Germany itself and still hit London. In fact, several dozen a day did hit the city.

The resulting disappointment was considerable, but it was somewhat misplaced. Actually there was no longer any question about who was going to win the war. In the battles across France and the Lowlands the Nazis had lost well over half a million men, many of them the best troops in the service, more than half of them in the form of prisoners, which is the most wasteful form of military expenditure since it inflicts no corresponding disabilities on the opponent. Another 150,000 Germans were locked up in the ports. Their reserve depots were empty; they were reduced to enlisting youths of fifteen and old men who had fought in the last war, to organizing Volksturm battalions of workers and women who had no military training. In the east, the Russians had for the first time conducted

a successful summer offensive, which cleared the whole Ukraine, old Poland, and Rumania; they were deep in Hungary on a thousand-mile front that required the full efforts of the depleted German armies merely to hold, and those armies were now back to a line they must maintain in order to keep intact the only remaining industrial areas beyond the range of Allied bombers. Worst of all, the Nazis had been unable to find any commander with the ability and freedom of action of Montgomery of the British, and among the Americans, of Patton, Bradley, and above all Eisenhower, whose campaign from June to September ranks as one of the greatest in military history.

CHAPTER XV

THE operations against Los Negros and Manus Islands of the Admiralty Group, 200 miles south of the great enemy base at Truk, had originally been scheduled for April, 1944, but were pushed up to the last day of February because the Japanese at Kwajalein and Truk, and those in the operations around Vitiaz Strait showed little disposition toward strategic counterattack. Manus was something more than another way station on the road along the New Guinea coast. It has an excellent harbor, well sheltered against weather, and, being remote from any land mass where Japanese bands were still afloat, did not require military operations in the hinterland. It was accordingly erected into a major base for southwest Pacific operations, the navy moving in floating repair shops, floating docks, depot ships and even bakeries afloat, while the army set up similar installations ashore.

Here were established the headquarters of the new Seventh Fleet, an organization headed by

Rear-Admiral Thomas C. Kinkaid, who had commanded in the battle of the Eastern Solomons in August, 1942. The organization was under General MacArthur's command and was intended to furnish naval support for operations primarily military, as Admiral Nimitz had been given four divisions of army troops for attacks on islands where the outlook and effect of the campaign would be fundamentally naval. For the time being, the new fleet consisted of escort carriers with destroyers and cruisers, heavy support being furnished by the fast battleship and carrier task forces from the Central Pacific. The service of information by means of code intercepts and submarine scouting had grown so efficient that there was little opportunity for the enemy to move heavy ships into the Southwest Pacific area without our forces being able to cut them off.

March and most of April, 1944, were spent in organizing the new base at Manus, shifting other base installations from Australia up to the cost of New Guinea, and preparing for the next move forward. This was to be Hollandia, 400 miles along the coast of New Guinea from the deepest previous penetration, an area isolated by a range of mountains that runs down from the central backbone of the island. Hollandia contained three excellent airfields and a harbor that could be erected into an advanced base. In those jungle countries information as to Japa-

nese strength was never wholly reliable and the
strategic importance of the place made it likely that
the enemy had concentrated there in force. Their
Eighteenth Army was known to be in New Guinea
and was supposed to be in the Hollandia area some
60,000 strong, with outer elements facing the Aus-
tralo-American forces just south of Medang. There
was an extensive barge traffic along the shore which
we never had been able to cut off completely,
though our light forces sank as many as a hundred
of these craft a month.

General MacArthur detailed all three divisions
of Lieutenant-General R. L. Eichelberger's I Corps
for the operation and, as it fell in the time gap of
Central Pacific operations between the taking of
Eniwetok and the major move against the Marianas, he besought the services of the fast carriers
for air support. The operation was thus the most
massive that had yet been undertaken in the Southwest Pacific. Cruisers and destroyers fired the preliminary bombardment on the night of April 21–
22; after dawn on the latter day landing forces
moved in simultaneously against the beaches of
Aitape and of Hollandia itself, preceded by intense
fire from rocket-gunboats.

Resistance was surprisingly light at both places.
By April 23 all the airfields were in American hands
and our fighters were being set up on the Aitape
air strip. The forces at the two landings worked

toward each other in a move to encircle the Japanese between coast and mountains, but only about a company of the enemy were cut off and exterminated. Their force had been overestimated; the rest of the less than five thousand men the area really held were driven off into the hills where most perished miserably without affecting the course of the war.

It was now clear that the majority of the New Guinea Japanese were in the Wewak area, but they were comparatively harmless there, blocked off from undertaking operations by the very combination of mountain and jungle that preserved them from landward attack. MacArthur began organizing his Hollandia base while some detachments pushed into the hills in pursuit of the Japanese there and others moved along the coast 75 miles to the next enemy station at the offshore island of Wakde, on which a landing was effected May 17. There was the usual fanatic resistance, overwhelmed with light casualties, for MacArthur had put in nearly an entire brigade against the single battalion of Japanese who held the island.

The next blow was made against Biak Island on May 27 by the 41st Division. The landing was made without opposition, but as our troops began to work along the coast road they ran into violent machine-gun and artillery fire from a line of bluffs, and were counterattacked by numbers of tanks

supported by infantry. Heavy fighting lasted
nearly a week; extra ships and planes had to be
brought in to support the beachhead and it became
evident that Biak was much more important in the
Japanese scheme of military economy than had
been supposed. The forces against the Japanese
were too powerful, however; their formal resistance
began to break on June 3. On June 6 one of the
airfields was reached and after that it was merely a
question of digging the remnants of the 8,000 enemy troops out of cave positions like those on
Saipan.

Early in July there was another landing at
Noemfor on the Vogelkop Peninsula in extreme
west New Guinea, followed on July 30 by one at
Sansapor, farther down the same peninsula. Both
of these caught the enemy off balance and achieved
their objectives with light loss. The New Guinea
campaign that had begun in June, 1943, was now
complete except for peripheral operations against
the Japanese still in the hills there, and at Wewak,
where a daily bombing and shelling from the sea
became the rule. The separate steps of this campaign have little of military interest and were much
alike—the swift rush of overwhelming forces to an
obscure beach, the hard labor to hack an air strip
out of the jungle, the assembly of troops and supplies for the next move. The real heroes of the
campaign were the medical and supply officers, and

the planners who achieved surprise against the enemy with a regularity that was almost monoto-
nous. In a little over a year they had changed
into a chain of American bases an area, 1,400 miles
long and occupied by nearly 250,000 enemy troops.

THOSE Japanese on Vogelkop Peninsula who escaped our attack retreated to the south face of the
island on Banda Sea and were evacuated by boat.
It was mid-August of 1944 before they were cleared
out and the new air strip at Sansapor brought into
full commission—about the same date that saw
Guam reconquered and the new bases in the Marianas operative. The conjunction of events brought
strategic considerations to the fore. Up to this time
the navy in the Central Pacific and General Mac-
Arthur in the South Pacific had conducted their
campaigns independently save when the fleet was
borrowed for some such operation as that against
Hollandia. It is probable that the navy would have
preferred to continue this arrangement. General
MacArthur had a well-known predilection for a return to the Philippines and a campaign there to
by-pass Japanese holdings in the Dutch Indies.
This would have the ancillary result of permitting
American naval operations in the South China Sea
and so cutting off the enemy's access to his sources
of supply in the south except by the undeveloped
and uncertain overland route through China.

The navy on the other hand would undoubtedly have preferred a campaign to cut off the Japanese lifeline more thoroughly and nearer the home islands at Formosa or some point in the Ryukyus, looking forward to a landing on the Chinese coast. But any conceivable move in that direction would involve a military campaign on a land mass of some size and would require many troops. MacArthur headed the only considerable body of troops in the South Pacific, and both for political reasons (it was a Presidential year) and the sentimental purpose of bringing aid to the Philippines at the earliest opportunity, the Joint Chiefs of Staff in Washington allowed the General's viewpoint to prevail. Troops and fleet were to operate together against the Philippines.

Troops and fleet had, however, swung far apart since the Solomons campaign. If the Philippines were to be attacked, it was necessary to bring them together again in an area where the expedition could be made up with reasonable security from enemy observation and where the fleet would still be in position to cover the new Central Pacific bases against any counterattack by Japanese mobile forces. Between our two commands stretched the vast belt of the Carolines, still held by the enemy in strength. Truk at its core was continually reinforced by airplanes staged out through the Philippines, and was itself used by the Japanese

reconnaissance planes that came down to look at the easternmost projection of MacArthur's advance.

These considerations fixed the point for the next offensive in the western Carolines. A base seized there would be even more forward than Sansapor and would be necessary for any attack on the Philippines. It was decided to take two bases. The MacArthur forces would attack Morotai off Halmahera, the air gate to the Indies, and the navy forces, simultaneously giving cover to the Morotai attack, would fall on Ulithi and the Palau group, then move on Yap. Halsey was placed in command of the forces afloat, which were again denominated the Third Fleet. Kinkaid remained attached to MacArthur, but with greatly augmented forces, which included most of the slow battleships available. They could be spared from the Third Fleet which now had eight of the new fast battleships in service with two more running their shakedown cruises.

The operations began on September 5 with a massive carrier strike against the Palaus, while cruisers and escort carriers of Halsey's command moved on Ulithi. The latter found no Japanese at the place and as it had an admirable sheltered lagoon it was decided to put the navy's train (floating base) in there. Meanwhile the cruisers and escort carriers pushed on to pick up the bombard-

ment of the Palaus where the fast battleships had left off, while the latter in turn moved on to give Morotai "the Halsey haircut," and then swung southwestward to attack the airfields in the eastern Philippines, from which the Japanese might be expected to attempt to support the areas now under pressure.

On the morning of September 8, Halsey's planes struck the fields of Mindanao. The Japanese warning system failed completely, many of their planes were caught on the ground, and off the coast they lost a whole convoy of ships. Halsey pounded the area for another day, then ran on to strike the air installations of Luzon. This time the Japanese were warned, for they had developed a radar system which gave them some service. There were air fights over the fields and over Manila harbor for two days; but if their information service had improved since our people last made contact with the Japanese, their aviation had gained nothing. From their scattered and inefficiently operated fields they could send up little to match the squadrons of nearly twenty carriers. As Halsey turned eastward on September 12, he left behind him the wreckage of nearly 2,000 Japanese planes. That night he sent through an urgent message suggesting that, since the Japanese proved so very weak in the Philippines, the attack on Yap be dropped out of the picture and the invasion of the islands be begun

as soon as Morotai and the Palaus were secure—a
reversal of the original plan, which had been to
invade after the winter rains were over.

THERE was a series of rapid-fire, long-range con-
ferences, in which Nimitz offered MacArthur the
services of three army divisions (the 7th, 77th,
and 96th) under navy control, for an immediate
invasion. The approval of the Joint Chiefs of Staff
was secured for the project. MacArthur had expected to have air support from Chennault's 14th
Air Force in South China. He was now informed
that this was impossible since the Japanese had
taken the bases, but the carriers made themselves
responsible for air cover till the General could win
fields for his own air force, the 5th. With this
background MacArthur agreed to speed up the invasion. It placed a burden of incredible weight and
complexity upon the staff planners who had so well
handled the New Guinea campaign, and it may
be said that, if the fate of the German war depended
on Eisenhower's Normandy invasion, the result of
the Japanese war was now wedded to this move.

The two new island invasions had taken place
on September 15, 1944, while the matter was still
being discussed, and furnished somewhat contra-
dictory indications as to the possibilities of success.
The actual landing on Morotai was unopposed.
The Japanese had evidently expected a move to

the shores of Halmahera across the strait and were disposed at the wrong place. The campaign thus consisted in hunting down a few scattered bands. The attack on the Palaus was directed against the two southernmost islands of the chain, Angaur and Peleliu. Part of the 81st Division attacked the former, the 1st Marine Division the latter, and it was assumed that if these two were gained, the larger islands of the group could be controlled from their air strips. Angaur was believed to be held by not more than a company of Japanese; Peleliu, by about 4,500 men.

The method was the same as that applied in the Marshalls. Carriers, battleships, and cruisers subjected the place to intensive bombardment for over a week before landing day. At Angaur the fighting was sharp but brief; in three days the island was clear. But Angaur lies outside the coral rim enclosing the atoll and has no harbor of its own. It was necessary to have Peleliu, and at Peleliu the Japanese demonstrated that their defensive techniques had caught up with our methods of attack. The island is a high structure of coral limestone honeycombed with caves; the Japanese had added to these and had built an intricate system of tunnels, linking cave to cave. The preliminary bombardments had hurt them very little. When the Marines hit the beach they were met by a storm of fire from pieces of all sizes which pinned them

down at once; they were then subjected to a tank-led counterattack that broke through one of our regiments.

It was far worse than the more publicized Tarawa operation, for each individual cave had to be cleared out in hand-to-hand fighting, and often enough the Japanese reoccupied the cave later by means of their interior tunnels. One of the Marine regiments lost two thirds of its numbers, the 81st Division had to be called on for help, and two months after the landing men were still being killed by snipers hidden underground.

This was clearly an instance of underestimating the enemy's strength and resources. On the other hand, it proved that Halsey had by no means underestimated their strength and resources in the air. After the Luzon strike, his fast ships ran up to the Marianas for a brief period of refueling and refitting and then turned into the Western Pacific toward the region of the Ryukyus and Formosa, the design being to knock out the planes with which the Philippines could be supported while those planes were still distributed among the reserve fields.

Halsey struck the fields of the southern Ryukyus on October 9, getting rid of a hundred Japanese machines and butchering a couple of small convoys without appreciable loss before he went on to strike the great bases of Formosa on the 11th, an attack

repeated the following day. The Japanese were comparatively well prepared. In a heavy air battle we lost 50 planes against 180 of theirs, and inflicted considerable damage on their shops and installations. That night they called in planes from the China coast or brought them out of underground hangars on Formosa and counterattacked the fleet; a night torpedo attack made in great force.

Against our night-fighter patrols and the gunfire of the fleet they succeeded in getting exactly one hit on a heavy cruiser, which was dragged home clear across the Pacific. But the determining factor of the battle was that, when shot down, the enemy planes exploded with such enormous violence among pillars of flame that many even of our own fighters thought several carriers had been blown up. The Japanese thoroughly believed it. Their messages (which we were decoding) announced the destruction of 11 American carriers.

Now Halsey's major concern was the Japanese fleet, and he believed he might persuade them out for a battle if he encouraged their delusion that they had destroyed so much of our carrier strength. Accordingly he turned south and east beyond range of Japanese scouts toward the Palaus with three of his four carrier groups. The fourth, that of Rear Admiral J. S. McCain, was left hovering in the great bight of ocean between Formosa and the

Philippines, flying a strike next morning against the fields of northern Luzon. McCain was duly attacked by torpedo planes again that night and the Japanese raised their count of American carriers sunk to fourteen. But they did not bring their fleet out and Halsey believed that his ruse had failed.

Now he ran down to join the Seventh Fleet in escorting the MacArthur armada, already on the water, toward the Philippines. At the last moment its destination had been changed from Mindanao, the point originally selected, to Leyte. The extremely active and well-informed guerrilla movement in the islands (it was supported by American submarines) sent out word that the Japanese had concentrated to the north and south of the Philippine group, leaving the central islands almost uncovered. On October 19, 1944, a Japanese search plane spotted the Seventh Fleet and the transports as they approached Leyte Gulf. On the 20th the landings began under cover of naval fire and rocket ships so effective that the first men on the beach (of the 1st Cavalry Division) penetrated half a mile into the jungles before they had a single casualty. General MacArthur returned to the Philippines during the morning, and army formations began to extend perimeters inland around the airstrips of Tacloban (Leyte's capital) and Dulag,

on which work began immediately. The Japanese resistance was light but persistent in that tangled country; the advance progressed slowly under cover of planes from the 18 escort carriers of Rear-Admiral Thomas Sprague, part of the Seventh Fleet. But before the military movements could attain the proportions of a campaign a new factor had entered the situation.

The Japanese fleet decided to fight. Halsey's stratagem had really deceived them, and when Rear-Admiral F. C. Sherman appeared in the bight of Luzon with a single carrier group on the 21st, the Japanese Admiral, Kurita, assumed it was the same group that had attacked Luzon on the 13th (McCain's) and that these were all the fast carriers we had left. The Japanese gunnery ships were in the region of Singapore; Kurita brought them north at speed along the western side of the Philippines. Two battleships, one heavy cruiser, and some light cruisers and destroyers were to run through the Sulu Sea into Surigao Strait and Leyte Gulf to attack our transports and beachheads. Five battleships, seven heavy cruisers, and a host of lighter craft were to run east through Sibuyan Sea and San Bernardino Strait, round Samar and so reach the same destination. Another cruiser and destroyer force was to start from the north through the Sulu Sea, and thence into Surigao Strait.

A force of 200 bombers, many of them suddenly

flown in from China, were to fly from the Luzon
fields and strike Sherman, while four carriers, all
that was left of that once great wing of the Japanese navy, with two battleships and many smaller
craft, ran down from the region of the Japanese
islands, well to the east. They were to fly their
planes across Sherman's ships, attacking as they
passed, to the landing fields of Luzon, then shuttle
back across the carriers again, to be picked up at
sea. These carriers were expected to be lost in de-
coying our ships away from Leyte Gulf. Finally,
the Japanese had organized a corps of pilots sworn
to dive into American ships with full bomb loads.
These—the Kamikaze—would attack the remnants
of the Seventh Fleet while Kurita's battleships were
pounding it.

This was the plan, many details of which did
not become clear to our side till much later. The
first word the American leaders had was on the
night of October 23, when our submarines *Darter*
and *Dace,* scouting off Dumaron Channel south of
Palawan, sighted Kurita's armada bound north.
They got the news off and attacked. In the most
successful submarine action of the whole war they
sank two of the Japanese heavy cruisers and sent
a third back to Singapore with four torpedo holes
in her. Halsey immediately moved his carrier
groups up to a point east of Samar and at dawn
on the 24th flew off search and strike groups. One

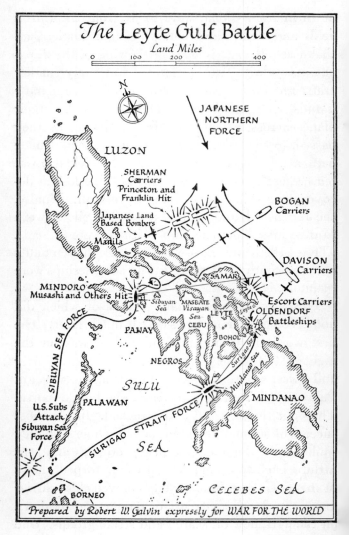

The Leyte Gulf Battle

Land Miles

0   100   200   400

N

JAPANESE
NORTHERN
FORCE

LUZON

SHERMAN
Carriers
Princeton and
Franklin Hit

BOGAN
Carriers

Japanese Land
Based Bombers

Manila

DAVISON
Carriers

SAMAR

MINDORO
Musashi and Others Hit

Sibuyan
Sea

MASBATE
Visayan
Sea

LEYTE

Escort Carriers
OLDENDORF
Battleships

PANAY

CEBU

BOHOL

NEGROS

Surigao Sea

SULU

Mindanao Sea

PALAWAN

MINDANAO

U.S. Subs
Attack
Sibuyan Sea
Force

SURIGAO STRAIT FORCE

SEA

BORNEO

CELEBES SEA

Prepared by Robert W. Galvin expressly for WAR FOR THE WORLD

of the strikes found a Japanese formation proceeding through Sulu Sea and inflicted some damage on it, but before a second strike could be flown
all planes were called to the northern end of the
area, where the much more important Japanese
force was steaming through Sibuyan Sea and Sherman's carrier group had been attacked by the land-
based bombers. Sherman beat off these attackers
with the loss of nearly a hundred enemy planes,
but not before they had left the light carrier *Princeton* furiously ablaze and had scored a hit on another carrier. He could give no help against the
Japanese battleships.

The other carrier groups attacked this force all
day, concentrating on the biggest ships, and cutting
them up very badly. In the final attack just at
twilight they set upon the battleship *Musashi,*
newest and finest of the Japanese navy, hitting her
so heavily that she sank before another dawn,
though our people did not know it at the time.
They were satisfied to see this battle force turning
west, back in the direction from which it had come.

Meanwhile Sherman's hard-pressed carriers had
been attacked by the Japanese planes coming in
from their carriers out to seaward. The *Princeton*
blew up and almost wrecked the light cruiser
Birmingham, which was helping her to put out
fires. The Japanese suffered considerably from our
air groups but a good portion of them got away.

So stood the situation on the night of October 24, 1944. One Japanese squadron was making through the Sulu Sea toward Surigao Strait at its best speed, with another coming to join it, the two admirals ignorant of each other. In the northern end of that strait, though the enemy did not know it, waited Rear-Admiral J. L. Oldendorf with six battleships of Kinkaid's command (five of them ships that had gone down at Pearl Harbor) and numerous cruisers and destroyers. In the Sibuyan Sea the main Japanese battle force was turning back after a dreadful battering from our carrier planes. On the Luzon fields, Japanese land-based and carrier bombers were reloading for another attack on Sherman's group, which they apparently still supposed were all the carriers we had left. Somewhere out to the north and east, not yet definitely located, was the Japanese carrier force with accompanying battleships.

During the night a long-range search plane from the Marianas found them, and Halsey turned toward them with his whole force. Some critics complained later that he had not left part of the ships to hold San Bernardino Strait, but it was old American tactical doctrine never to divide a fleet in the presence of an enemy. It will also be remembered that no one on the American side yet knew how extensive the Japanese losses in the June battle (Philippine Sea) had been. Instead of its actual

size of one large and three light carriers, this Japanese force might easily have contained five of each type, and if so, it was by far the most formidable opponent. Halsey hurried toward it through the dark at his best speed. The decoy thus was a success.

In that same dark at about 3:00 A.M. the southernmost Japanese force entered Surigao Strait. Oldendorf had disposed his battleship across the exit of the strait with cruisers and destroyers down both sides. As soon as his radar showed the enemy steaming straight on in line ahead, his destroyers let loose shoals of torpedoes and the heavy ships opened up a torrent of gunfire rarely seen in war —*Tennessee* alone fired 69 shells of a ton weight and 63 of them hit. In twelve minutes the entire Japanese squadron was reduced to a group of floating wrecks, with damage to only one of the destroyers on our side. A little later the second enemy force arrived and was as badly hurt.

But still worse was in store for the Japanese. At daybreak Halsey's planes found the carrier force. Its planes (as we have seen) had left it to fly into Luzon and no defense remained but anti-aircraft fire with which to oppose the heaviest carrier attack yet seen in the Pacific. One of their carriers went down under that first blow. All the rest of the ships were more or less badly hit and turned to race back toward Japan as fast as they were able.

But before a second strike could be flown to finish them, before the American battleships could close in with their big guns, the radio brought Halsey an appalling piece of news. The Japanese Sibuyan Sea force, with which he thought he had finished, had turned again during the night, speeded up, burst through San Bernardino Strait, and now had Sprague's escort carriers under its guns, with Leyte Gulf, crowded with transports, only a little beyond.

It seemed that nothing could save those escort carriers. They were armorless and slow, converted from merchant hulls. Their only cover was a handful of destroyers and destroyer escorts. The range was point blank. Oldendorf was far distant, with slow ships now nearly out of both fuel and ammunition. The destroyers and destroyer escorts made smoke screens and gallantly attacked with the torpedo. Three of them (*Johnston, Hoel, Roberts*) were sunk, and the escort carrier *Gambier Bay* took an engine-room hit that caused her to drop back among the onrushing Japanese and go down under their gunfire. But all the Japanese ships had been severely battered by carrier planes the day before and this damage had fallen particularly upon their upper works where range finders and fire-control instruments were located. Their gunnery was wretched. Moreover, the escort carriers themselves were by no means helpless. Their own planes took off to fall on the Japanese in attack after

attack. In one of these rushes they sank the heavy cruiser *Suzuyu* with seven torpedo hits and hit another cruiser so badly that she was forced to turn away. At about 9:30, after two hours of firing, being short of ammunition and having suffered dismaying losses, the rest of the Japanese imitated her, realizing that before they could finish the escort carriers Halsey and his whole armada would be down on them.

Halsey had indeed turned back, leaving Admiral Mitscher with one group of carriers to complete the work on the Japanese force in the north, but rejecting the latter's plea to give him a couple of battleships, the only action for which the American fleet commander can really be blamed. His planes ran ahead to the neighborhood of Samar. Sometime around noon or a little after, they charged head on into the few remaining Japanese carrier planes coming out from Luzon to rejoin their own fleet, of whose disaster they had not yet heard. The enemy were in no condition to combat the overwhelming American fighter groups and were nearly all shot down.

About the same time the Kamikaze attacked the escort carriers, just delivered from the Japanese battleships, and though most were shot down, one of them did crash through the deck of the escort carrier *St. Lo,* setting fires that could not be checked. Halsey's air-strike groups pressed on, hit-

ting the Japanese now in flight through San Bernardino Strait and slowing them up enough so that our battleships caught one or two ships and finished them off. In the north, Mitscher's men flew two more major strikes against the Japanese carrier group fleeing for home. All their carriers were sunk and all their other ships crippled. In the night an American submarine got one of their cruisers; for three days more our carrier planes hunted all over the Philippines, finding and sinking damaged destroyers, and within the week two more injured heavy cruisers had been sent down in the bays of Luzon where they had taken refuge.

That was the Battle of Leyte Gulf, the greatest in American naval history. In that confused series of actions the Japanese carrier service had been wiped out, together with 392 airplanes; three of their battleships had been sunk; they had lost eight of their twelve heavy cruisers (two after the battle itself), five light cruisers and nine destroyers— more than half their navy, which never again operated as a fleet, for the remaining five battleships and four heavy cruisers were badly hurt. To the war in the Pacific, Leyte was what St. Lô-Avranches had been to the war in Europe—the crushing blow. After it, the enemy could have no higher hope than a negotiated peace which would leave them some fragments of their empire.

CHAPTER XVI

RECONQUEST OF THE PHILIPPINES

As captured documents later showed, the Japanese were completely deceived by General MacArthur's landing on Leyte in October, 1944. They had expected a two-pronged attack—from the Central Pacific forces under Nimitz against northern Luzon and from MacArthur's men at Mindanao. The virtual destruction of their fleet in Leyte Gulf accordingly left them in very poor position, without any good means of assembling at the point of contact the 350,000 men who formed the garrison of the islands.

Their commander, Terauchi, nevertheless decided to fight for Leyte, since the island's central mountain range had few passes and they could be held by relatively small forces. Where the country was open it was largely in rice paddies, and the season of torrential rains was at hand. These were all factors that favored a static defense and cut down American mobility, while the water channels among the islands west of Leyte were narrow

enough to permit considerable supporting movement in small craft by night, when our aviation was
least effective. (The fact that both Japanese and
Germans were forced to seek positions from which
American mobility could be discounted was not
accidental but the product of two perfectly measurable military factors, the exceptional power of
movement conferred on our forces by their automo-
tive equipment, which could bring supplies up so
rapidly, and the operations of our air force, which
made rapid movement so difficult for the opponents.)

General MacArthur's problem was the converse
of the Japanese—to break out rapidly from the area
in which he was penned between the beach and
mountains of Leyte and, using the strategic mobility conferred by our command of the sea, to deal
with the enemy forces in detail. He had six divisions in the Sixth Army of General Kreuger—not
over 100,000 men—with the support of General
Kenney's Fifth Air Force after the Dulag and Tacloban strips were set up and others added. General
Walter Kreuger had already demonstrated, and
would so again, that he was one of the ablest American commanders anywhere in the field; he was a
German immigrant, gifted with wonderful persist-
ence, a skillful tactician whose greatest recommen-
dation was nevertheless not tactics but his control
of morale by living like his soldiers and treating

their problems as his own. "We all command armies," he told a meeting of sergeants once, "the only difference being that mine is larger than yours." He also had the support of Halsey's planes from the fast carriers, which were used for this purpose because practically all the Seventh Fleet escort carriers had been disabled in the battle of October 24–25.

Four days after that date, on October 29, the plain of eastern Leyte had been cleared to the mountains and the 1st Cavalry Division had secured the southern tip of Samar, where it abuts on that plain across a very narrow strait. In frantic efforts to hold the American forces back, the Japa-

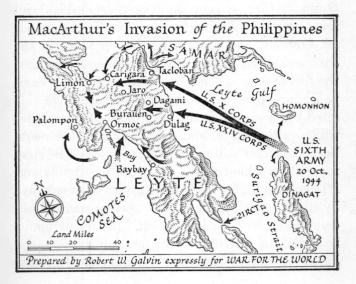

MacArthur's Invasion of the Philippines

Prepared by Robert W. Galvin expressly for WAR FOR THE WORLD

nese had spent a whole division, wiped out in piecemeal attacks with over 14,000 killed, while our
casualties were under 3,000. The X Corps of the
Sixth Army now moved to the north coast to get
around the mountains by one of the two good roads
at that flank, while the XXIV Corps took a road
through a good pass southward leading to Baybay.
It was slow and dificult work at both ends of the
line, thanks to the continual rains, but the Japanese
were too inferior at every point of contact to make
a really good defense, and by November 2 the
XXIV Corps had broken through to Baybay with a
foothold on the west coast.

By this time the enemy had set up his base at
Ormoc farther north on the same coast and had elements of four divisions in there, one of them their
1st Division, supposed to be the very best in the
Japanese service; their presence made it clear that
the Japanese were committing themselves to a campaign for Leyte. All the enemy divisions had suffered considerably from the attacks of our planes
while on the water, and now their reinforcements
began to suffer still more. The capture of Baybay
made it possible to base American destroyers and
PT-boats in Ormoc Bay and to attack their convoys
by night as well as day. This service was not accomplished without loss to our side, for at night,
free from the attentions of American fighters, the
Japanese planes attacked constantly. But the

enemy lost so heavily in troops that they had difficulty building up large-scale organizations and were
constantly forced to expend men and materials in
local emergency operations that achieved no more
than small-area delays. The disorganization became so pronounced that MacArthur's headquarters somewhat prematurely announced on November 7 that another two weeks would see the island
won.

At the end of November the X Corps had taken
Limon at the head of the valley which leads south
to Ormoc, but the XXIV Corps, moving up from
the south toward Ormoc, was substantially halted
at a defensible river line, and a division that had attempted to work across the island in the center by
mountain trails was making little progress. Mac-
Arthur got his 77th Division into light transports
and, after a violent air-sea combat that lasted all
the night of December 6–7, put them ashore in
Ormoc Bay, just north of the Japanese-held river
line. This broke up the enemy positions in both
directions, and though they did a good deal of damage by dropping suicide parachutists onto our airfields on the night of December 8 their forces
rapidly dissolved. On December 21 the last organized resistance broke. The total enemy casualty list
was 55,000 men, all but 493 of them killed; our
casualties were 11,000. Obscure, semi-guerrilla
fighting continued among the hills for nearly six

months more, in the course of which another 22,000 Japanese were killed, almost none surrendering. Marshal Terauchi fled to Saigon in Indo-China.

On December 13, 1944, after it became evident that the Ormoc Bay landing would succeed in breaking down the enemy on Leyte, a force of transports under heavy naval escort carried a combat team, two regiments strong, right through the Central Philippines to the coast of Mindoro, the large island just south of Luzon. They rapidly gained all essential areas without meeting any Japanese force of more than constabulary strength. The operation was both an experiment and a preparation; the former because the convoy had to move through narrow waters after having been observed from the outset by the enemy, the latter because it was necessary to establish a forward base before undertaking the invasion of Luzon, most important of the Philippine islands.

The Japanese attacked the convoy continuously from the air during the two nights it was on the water, but all through the month of November Kenney's air force had been hammering at their installations throughout the central islands and the damage inflicted on the convoy was insignificant. The way was accordingly clear for the main attack. It was preceded by a series of feints that succeeded in persuading the Japanese commander that Mac-

The Luzon Campaign

Land Miles
0 25 50 100

Vigan

Aparri

Tuguegarao

Lingayen Gulf

U.S. I CORPS

U.S. XIV CORPS

U.S. SIXTH ARMY
9 Jan., 1945

Baguio

Dagupan

6686

U.S. XI CORPS
29 Jan., 1945

Subic Bay

BATAAN

Mariveles

Corregidor

31 Jan., 1945

Lubang Is.

Nasugbu

Balayan Bay

Batangas Bay

VERDE

CLARK FIELD

Olongapo

LUZON

Manila Bay

MANILA

Cavite

Laguna de Bay

Polillo Islands

Lamon Bay

PHILIPPINE SEA

MINDORO

San José

15 Dec., 1944

Mindoro Strait

Tayabas Bay

MARINDUQUE

SIBUYAN SEA

PANAY

MASBATE

Ragay Gulf

San Miguel Bay

6483

Lagonoy Gulf

Legaspi

1 April, 1945

San Bernardino Strait

SAMAR

Prepared by Robert W. Galvin expressly for WAR FOR THE WORLD

Arthur meant to land in the Batangas area south of Manila. Mine sweepers moved into the bays there and cleared them out under heavy gunnery cover, planes dropped dummies to simulate an airborne invasion, and several times transports moved in. Meanwhile Filipino guerrillas and the air forces vigorously attacked transportation bottlenecks on Luzon at bridges and ravines. This campaign of confusion was highly successful, for the Japanese, both deceived and uncertain, suffered serious road jams, parceled out their strength needlessly, and had neither good defenses at the shore nor centralized reserves when the real blow fell. With the exception of a single division at some distance, every unit of the close to 200,000 men the Japanese had in the island was on the march in some direction on January 9, 1945, when our troops hit the beach.

The place was the east shore of Lingayen Gulf. The units were of the Sixth Army, now composed of the I and XIV Corps with a completely different list of divisions than when, as nominally the same force, it had struck the beaches of Leyte. The gunnery support was provided by all the vessels of the Seventh Fleet and most of those of the Third Fleet. This proved to be nothing less than necessary, for as the ships moved into Lingayen Gulf it became clear that there was more than one reason why the Japanese aerial counterattacks had tapered off earlier. They had withdrawn many of their planes

from service to convert them into Kamikaze, the suicide attackers, and as these planes were not expected to return, they could be operated from otherwise inefficient and easily concealed air strips.

The Kamikaze began their attacks on January 6, as soon as the invasion fleet of over 800 vessels was in easy range. They came in at twilight or dawn in groups close to the water, so that the protecting fighters found it difficult to deal with them and there was some danger of hitting our own ships with gunfire. The attacks were made in unexpected strength and so achieved considerable results. An escort carrier was sunk, and also three mine sweepers. So many other vessels were damaged with great loss of life that the abandonment of the whole operation was seriously considered. Instead Halsey took his Third Fleet north for a great strike on Formosa, hitting the airfields there so effectively that there was little interference with the actual process of landing except from a few pieces of light artillery, easily disposed of.

Once the troops began to reach shore the picture began to change rapidly and radically. The Japanese, like the Germans before them, expected our forces to strike first for one of the ports. They were, therefore, caught so badly out of position that by twilight of the first day 68,000 men were ashore on a beachhead 15 miles long and three miles deep. The flanks were extended rapidly in both direc-

tions, but it was January 15 before any important enemy forces were found, and these on the extreme northeastern flank around Rosario, where the Japanese brought up a few pieces of heavy artillery to shell the beachhead from long range. General MacArthur put his weight out toward this flank and succeeded in getting a strong grip on both the main highways that led from Manila up the central valley of Luzon before the two divisions the Japanese had sent north could arrive.

The Japanese by the middle of January did succeed in getting a considerable force into the hill country east of this main valley, their heaviest concentration being on the north flank. This was fairly close to the landing beaches across which our forces were still getting their supplies. The American General put his I Corps out to this flank among the foothills to prevent any counterattack against his communications, and with his XIV Corps pushed rapidly south along the valley toward Manila. It was expected that the enemy would make a stand in the highly defensible position where the River Agno swings a big bend across the valley. Preparations were made for a battle at that point. The event showed that the confusion of Japanese councils and the disarray of their communications had been underestimated rather than the reverse, and MacArthur's advance through the central plain found only weak rear guards at the

Agno. The first heavy fighting came at Clark Field on January 25. The Japanese were found strongly dug in around the field itself and even more firmly entrenched in the hills behind it, from which they could keep the field under artillery fire and prevent its use.

General MacArthur accordingly had to send a considerable force westward into the Zambales Mountains, as he had previously thrust the whole I Corps eastward, where it had encountered strong resistance and was several times counterattacked during January. But these counterattacks were local and piecemeal, and the American leader gave his opponents no time to assemble a mass of maneuver that might take advantage of the weakening of his main column by detachments to the flanks.

On January 9 he put the XI Corps of the Eighth Army ashore on the west coast of Bataan Peninsula near Subic Bay, from whence they pushed rapidly across the peninsula to link up with and to strengthen the main drive. Two days later the 11th Airborne Division went ashore at Nasugbu on Batangas Peninsula south of Manila. When the Japanese attempted to move forces forward to hold off this new attack, the 11th leapfrogged over them in a parachute movement on February 4 and cut these forces off. That same day advance elements of the I Corps reached the northern outskirts of Manila, and now from all directions our troops

came pouring down to close the circuit, laying the place under effective siege by February 7.

THE campaign for Luzon was over by February of 1945, but the fighting had hardly begun. The skill of MacArthur's deceptions and the swiftness of his moves were aided enormously by sure information from the Philippine guerrillas as to every Japanese disposition, and also by our command of the sea, which enabled him to strike anywhere in a country whose lines of communication all run close to the water. As a result of these factors, the Japanese were left without a strategy. They were condemned to a defense which consisted in assembling troops in the roughest ground near their stations and waiting to be attacked.

After the American forces closed around Manila on February 7, our troops faced four such main groups, of varying size. The most important was in the mountains of the bulging northern peninsula, now under attack along its perimeter by troops of the I Corps. A somewhat smaller but still important groupment was holding out in the Zambales Mountains and Bataan Peninsula, west of the central valley of Luzon; a third was in the hills around Fort McKinley east of Manila. All three of these were fairly active and made frequent local counter-attacks, but were limited to night operations by the presence of our light planes which flew constantly

over their positions at tree-top level, bringing down artillery fire on everything that moved.

The fourth concentration was in Manila city itself, with a strong garrison on Corregidor rock in the bay, and it was toward this that General Mac-Arthur first directed his attention, partly because of the moral importance of the place, but principally to gain the use of Manila harbor. Three divisions were put in against the city itself, while two more attacked the forces in the mountains eastward. The latter made good progress at the beginning, cutting all of the communications between the enemy force here and the one in northern Luzon.

The fighting in Manila turned into a desperate inch-by-inch, house-to-house struggle, in which the Japanese killed many of the native inhabitants, mined everything, and made frequent suicide charges on a small scale. By February 21 the area north of the Pasig River, which splits Manila in half, had been cleared and General MacArthur announced that the city was ours. The announcement was premature because the Japanese had dug themselves into the old walled stone city south of the river. A major operation by the full strength of two divisions, with enormous air and artillery support, was necessary to dislodge them, a task not accomplished till the end of the month. The city was left in ruins, without sanitary facilities or

utilities; great difficulty was experienced in preventing epidemics.

Meanwhile, Bataan had been cleared by the 38th Division, which landed at the tip of the peninsula on February 15 and worked rapidly around the north shore of Manila Bay. Corregidor, under intense bombardment since January 23, fell on February 16 to a parachute attack, admirably timed to arrive at the same moment as a seaborne landing. The remaining Japanese defenders blew themselves up in the tunnels of the Rock to a number never accurately determined; over 4,000 bodies were found aboveground. Another island fortress, Fort Drum, was too small and rugged to be attacked by such means and the Japanese in the place were not eliminated until ships moved up and pumped into its structure vast quantities of gasoline which was then set afire.

From this point on, the fighting on Luzon becomes somewhat obscure because all its separate battles were on a small scale and lacking in interest except to the men who fought in them. Both in the Zambales Mountains and east of Manila the Japanese succeeded in getting into positions with systems of interconnecting caves not unlike those on Peleliu. The position east of Manila was particularly difficult and irritating, since from it the enemy controlled the water reservoirs which constituted the city's supply. Although General MacArthur wanted

this and some of the other positions badly enough to make certain sacrifices, there was no such immediate urgency as that which had made the bloody attacks on Peleliu and Saipan a necessity. The war therefore proceeded slowly, on an almost purely tactical level, with the elimination of each position being treated as a separate engineering problem.

In the solution of these problems the most general method was to work men forward to seal the mouth of each cave with explosive charges. Most of the country was too rough for the use of tanks. Artillery fire, rockets, and the new recoilless gun were constantly used to provide covering fire. The Japanese retorted by constant small-scale counterattacks and a campaign of harassments. In spite of the hopelessness of their position, they almost never surrendered. Their efforts were directed toward wearing out the patience of our soldiers and inflicting more casualties on us than they themselves suffered. In the first of these objectives they achieved some success, as later events were to demonstrate, though none that affected the war. The second attempt was an abject failure. General MacArthur's orders to his operations officers were that no attack was to be attempted unless it gave fair promise of ten Japanese casualties for every American. This was not always attained, since our forces occasionally met surprises in the strength or nature of an

enemy position, but the actual figure seldom passed below five for one.

In fighting of this character all the east and south of Luzon were cleared during the spring and Baguio was taken, the summer capital and the only place where the Japanese attempted a formal battle. In June, General Kreuger's forces drove into the wide Cagayan Valley, which splits northern Luzon in half. Parachute forces, Philippine guerrillas, and a seaborne attack took Aparri on the north coast, cutting the Japanese from their last contact with the homeland even by submarine and, driving southward, split the remainder of the enemy into pockets.

The supporting fleet had suffered badly during a typhoon in September, 1944, when three destroyers foundered and many other ships were damaged. As soon as Manila Bay was opened to provide a secure anchorage where an expedition could be organized without the necessity of carrying it across Pacific distances, the attack was spread to the other islands of the archipelago. This movement opened on the last day of February, when a combat team from the 41st Division attacked Puerto Princessa on Palawan, the best harbor in the southwestern Philippines. They took it from light opposition, most of the Japanese retreating to the interior hills. Early in April other detachments of the same division took Jolo and Tawitawi in the extreme southern

Philippines, the objective being to gain the key harbors at this end of the vast Philippine group and to cut off from the enemy whatever fitful communication, by means of a small craft, he still had with Borneo and the Japanese-held islands to the south.

On March 10 still another team of the 41st made a beginning on the great island of Mindanao, with a landing at Zamboanga at its extreme western tip. There was hard fighting there, but as on Palawan the matter was not pushed for the moment beyond the seizure of a port and a defensive perimeter. The situation on that big island was militarily peculiar. It contained powerful Japanese forces, but the Philippine guerrilla movement, here in the hands of the warlike Moros, was so strong and well ed that not long after the Leyte fighting the enemy were pinned down to a few fortified areas and practically deprived of the power of movement; a considerable portion of the northern part of the island was in control of the insurgents. Elements of General R. L. Eichelberger's Eighth Army were engaged in clearing the central Philippines during March and early April against opposition that was generally weak. Now on April 17 the whole X Corps was put ashore at Cotaboto on the western face of the main mass of Mindanao. It expediously drove eastward through the valleys to Davao, the main Japanese center in the south,

which was reached early in May. There was hard house-to-house fighting here, of the same type as at Manila, with the Japanese ultimately borne down by numbers and artillery fire.

The X Corps turned north, fanning out along several lines of communication, and simultaneously more troops were landed at Agusan in the guerrilla-held north. The Mindanao operation now took on the same character as that in Luzon—a painstaking searching out and reduction of enemy cave positions (where these did not exist the Japanese made them), whose requirements were chiefly time and ammunition.

When the operation ended there were over 317,000 Japanese dead in the Philippines and they had yielded 7,000 prisoners; the total American casualties (four fifths of them were wounded men who would recover) were 60,000. Such statistics tell more eloquently than any words the tale of a campaign in which an enemy with over-all numerical superiority was outmaneuvered and outgunned at every point through sound strategy and adroit use of the forces of air and sea.

Yet even this does not explain the complete failure of the Japanese to make any effective defense their inability to bring anything but endurance and devotion to the business of war. The fact is that their whole military system had been based on too rigid an obedience to orders, in which there was no

room for initiative on the part of commanders in the field; and on a system of "military honor" which forbade subordinates to inform their superiors that orders had not been carried out. This was neatly illustrated in the Leyte campaign. Marshal Terauchi's orders were to hold the pass at the north end of the island against the American advance while reinforcements sufficient to drive the invaders into the sea were brought through Ormoc. Neither the over-all commander at the pass nor any of his subordinates reported that post after post was falling to our attack; the commander of the reinforcing formation continued to move his transports while the American destroyers and planes were making it obviously impossible to get more than a small percentage through; and the official documents still showed the Japanese position as good, when in fact it had become desperate.

Again, all the formations in movement on the roads of Luzon when MacArthur's blow fell continued to move until they had reached their destinations and then had to be moved back again, arriving too late. Some of the Japanese local commanders knew of the attack, but their system did not allow them to act until they had received orders from above.

CHAPTER XVII

THE EUROPEAN ENEMY BREAKS

AFTER the battle lines became stabilized along the Scheldt and the frontiers of Germany in September, 1944, and the effort to outflank the enemy defensive position on the north had failed, the most important objective before the Allied High Command was the improvement of its logistic position to the point where a general assault on the Nazi defensives could be undertaken. In this question was comprehended not only the matter of bringing up supplies, which is the usual province of logistics, but also a variety of others reaching back to the sources of supply in the United States. The expenditure of artillery shells, for instance, had been far heavier than anticipated, and grave errors had been made in the War Department in ordering the types of shell needed. These errors had to be rectified, and before this was done some shortages were felt at the front during the autumn battles. The needs for replacements among combat infantry had been far underestimated, and as the Selective Service System lagged well behind the requirements in

producing them, many men had to be combed out of the various specialized formations.

But the foremost necessity was that of finding new ports through which supplies already existing could be brought to the battle line. Antwerp was chosen as the best available, both because of its excellent and intact dock facilities and because its use meant a shorter haul to reach the northern end of the long fighting line where the main actions would obviously be taking place. To open Antwerp it was necessary to gain control of the islands at the mouth of the Scheldt, an operation undertaken in mid-October by Marshal Montgomery's British and Canadian forces, with a heavy attack north from the region of Antwerp and an operation in a northwesterly direction against the causeway to the island of South Beveland.

The fighting was desperate, progress was slow, and casualties were very heavy, but the island was conquered on October 30, and a campaign was then begun for the reduction of the other island, Walcheren. An attempt to flood the Germans out by cutting the dikes failed; the attack had to be undertaken as an amphibian operation which, as expected, proved costly in the extreme; nevertheless it was completed by November 9. As soon as mines were cleared from the river, ships began to use Antwerp, but the enemy retorted by opening an intensive fire of V-1 buzz-bombs against the city,

which was still within easy range of the emplacements at the border. Antwerp was frightfully battered, receiving a far heavier bombardment from these weapons than London in earlier days. Liège also, as the chief communications center behind our front, was subjected to an intense fire of pilotless missiles, which caused much damage and many casualties. But the overall supply situation was eased.

MEANWHILE, the operations on the American portion of the front had become a war of position. For the whole central sector the key was the city of Metz, upon which all the roads and railroads from Lorraine and the Palatinate converge, so that its possession by the enemy gave him an effective block on movement in any direction. Early in October, 1944, a direct assault on Metz by General Patton's Third Army forces failed, and the breakdown contributed not a little to the general depression at this time. It was then decided to pinch the place out by an envelopment from both flanks at a distance beyond the range of the fortress guns.

The attack was opened on November 1 north of Nancy, as a local operation in rough ground to clear assembly areas and artillery positions from which more extensive attacks could be launched. It did not attract the attention of the Germans, who left the matter to their local reserves, and the necessary positions were gained without too severe a struggle.

The 9th Air Force, which had been set up in France to give the armies closer coöperation than could be provided by the 8th from England, now began a systematic attack on German communications throughout Lorraine. This continued for a week, more or less advertising the attack northeast of Nancy, which was opened on November 7 and immediately met by the enemy with strong counterattacks. On the first day there was little gain against these but the Germans were much hurt by our artillery fire. On November 8 they began to yield ground and in very hard fighting were pressed back south of Metz to the ring of forts round the city itself.

November 9 saw the opening of the offensive north of the city, where the problem was to cross the swift and steep-banked Meuse. Patton made great use of armor in the early stages and won a pair of good bridgeheads on either side of Thionville, but the operation became an infantry affair when the Nazis in turn put in armor. Our tanks were not at all adapted to battle the better-armored and better-gunned German tanks, and the wooded country of Lorraine, with its narrow valleys, offered little room for the swift sweeping advances for which the American machines were intended. South of Thionville the infantry advance, with strong artillery support, broke into the ring of Metz forts on November 14 and captured some of them, find-

ing evidence of enemy disorganization in the fact that few were properly supplied with ammunition and some did not have all their guns in position.

The next day the Germans tried an amored counterattack with a whole panzer division, but the attack had been anticipated and was completely broken up. This really sealed the fate of the great fortress. So many of its supporting roads were now either in our hands or under our fire that a break anywhere in the line would cut it off. The Germans retreated along the whole front to approximately the line of the frontier, where mountain ridges with their own newer and better-designed fortifications gave them superior positions for defense. Some of the Metz forts continued to hold out with small garrisons till mid-December; after that the place became an American communications center.

Farther north the great sweep of the summer had carried through Belgium and Luxembourg with hardly a check till it reached the German frontier. Here our First Army (Hodges) was in position next to the Third, with the Ninth (Simpson) being gradually built into the line between it and the British, all facing east along the Belgian border. These constituted the Twelfth Army group, under Bradley's command. The key of the line at this point was the city of Aachen, a road center like Metz, and of paramount importance because through it lay the only routes by which the German

plains could be reached without campaigning through ridge after ridge of fortified hills as in the south, or reaches of inundated flats, as farther north. The objective was the plain leading to Cologne; secondarily, the mining district of the Saar.

American forces reached the place on September 3 and got into the outer edge of Aachen but could make no further progress and were driven out by a German rally. Although small territorial gains were made, attempts at encirclement north and south of the town broke down in heavy fighting during early October, as did a direct attack after an aerial bombardment rivaling that of Cassino. Antwerp was not yet open at this date and the enemy could reinforce more rapidly than we could. They showed no hesitation in using their tactically superior armor, and in the stone-built town the air bombs only created rubble heaps which the more effectively protected cellar positions where the defenders were dug in around their guns. There was an organizational pause while fresh units of the Ninth Army were moved into position. Then General Hodges began the systematic reduction of each strong point in turn, using, principally, self-propelled guns protected against return fire by a host of other batteries. The operations north and south of Aachen put our artillery in position to cut off supply and reinforcement, and on October 21 Aachen surrendered.

Some distance to the east, the small river Roer courses through a double line of hills in a direction mainly northward, but beyond these hills a fairly open plain extends to Cologne and the banks of the Rhine. The hills and the towns along the Roer had been worked into the Siegfried defensive system. Their long stand in Aachen had given the Germans opportunity to move in new artillery and to improve these positions in the light of experience, an opportunity which they did not neglect. Their general method was to provide a wide variety of concreted gun positions with protected approaches and to move self-propelled artillery into each in turn for a few salvos, withdrawing before counteraction could be taken. The weather had now become so very unfavorable that air operations were severely limited. The Antwerp supply line was not yet in efficient operation. Nevertheless General Eisenhower decided on a winter campaign against this flank of the enemy defenses.

He had several reasons for this decision. One was that the Nazis were evidently in grave difficulties about reserves. They had instituted a combing-out process in home industry, converted many lines-of-communication troops into fighting units, and enlisted a vast "peoples' army" to make good the losses they had suffered in France and on the Russian front. But all these new units required training, and, if they could be forced into open field

operations before this training was complete, we would have every advantage. Another reason was the known unwillingness of the Germans to conduct winter campaigns, together with the fact that the Russian front had been quiescent since September. If the Nazis could be forced to fight all winter they would have to meet a massive Soviet spring offensive with men exhausted by warfare under the hardest conditions, instead of with units that would ordinarily have spent several months in rest areas. Finally, ground existed for believing that the German scientists were near success with weapons far more deadly than V-1 or V-2, and there was at least a chance that one of these might succeed in changing the whole face of the war unless the Germans could first be defeated in the field.

It had been many years since northern Europe experienced a winter so unfavorable to military operations as that encountered by our troops when they began their offensive on November 1, 1944; icy rains, freezing mud, and low clouds kept our air forces grounded for most of the day and interfered with artillery observation. The warfare was strictly one of positions. The British attacked in the north to clear whatever pockets the Germans still had west of the Maas and to support the left flank of the direct frontal assault undertaken by the Ninth and First armies together. In Lorraine the Third

and Seventh armies edged forward slowly to keep the Germans from moving reserves. It was dogged and extremely hard fighting. Gains were limited to a few hundred yards a day and frequently were canceled by counterattacks. The capture of each stone village or pillbox became a separate operation; all fighting was on a purely tactical level. The favorable features were that the Germans were forced to commit reserves they would have preferred to withhold; and as some of these reserves were very green formations with only six weeks of training, and as our aerial attacks on their communications kept up unremittingly, their casualties were far higher than ours.

Early in December the banks of the Roer were reached at two or three points, and now a new difficulty appeared. There was a system of dams at the headwaters of that stream. If the sluices were suddenly opened the resulting flash flood would be fatal to any attempt to cross the stream. While an effort was undertaken to reduce the bridgehead on the west bank which the Germans still held at Düren, another offensive was undertaken in a southeasterly direction into the wild country between Monschau and Schmidt to obtain possession of the dams. This was gaining slowly when an entirely new factor entered the campaign.

After the signal defeats in France, Hitler had restored Marshal Rundstedt to the command of his

armies in the west. Their success in holding our forces at the frontier owed much to his organizing and strategic ability. Early in December, under direct orders from Hitler, he began preparing the first winter offensive undertaken by a German army since Frederick the Great.

By such devices as stripping the garrisons of Norway and Czechoslovakia, a force of 24 divisions, mostly below full strength, was assembled opposite the frontier of Luxembourg and that part of Belgium which adjoins it on the north. German communications in this area were none too good, but those on our side of the line were very bad indeed, for here lies the rugged region of the Ardennes, now deep in snow. We could not quickly reinforce against an attack. Once a German advance crossed this region it would reach Liège, the main communication center for all the armies in the north, with Givet and Dinant on the Meuse where, as the Germans knew, we had vast stores of fuel, food, and ammunition. If these points were reached, the drive would become self-sustaining. The attackers fully counted on its doing so and at least reaching Antwerp with the resultant cutting off of all the Allied armies in the north. Thus, as the Germans moved forward to the attack on December 16, their propagandists shouted that they would be back in Paris by Christmas.

They very nearly made it. So many of the First

Army's troops had been drawn into the fighting
along the Roer that a great part of the front opposite the attack was held by a new division without
battle experience, the 106th. It was cut to pieces
in the first rush. Our High Command had noted
the German concentration, but had estimated that
it was intended for counterattack against the flanks
of our own movement toward Cologne, since it consisted mainly of infantry, our intelligence having
failed to note the presence of two fresh and strong
armored divisions brought in from Norway. The
enemy used parachutists in great numbers, many
of them in American uniforms, against our lines
of communication. Heavy fogs protected them
from our air forces. In three days the attack
had gone 20 miles into our lines and had taken
prisoners equal to the strength of a division. Communications were disorganized throughout the
whole Ardennes triangle.

General Eisenhower reacted with speed and
vigor. A corps was drawn from the British to hold
Liège and the northern part of the line of the
Meuse. The American First Army as well as the
Ninth were placed under Montgomery's command
since he could more conveniently control their
movements from the north side of the break, and he
vigorously counterattacked that shoulder of the
penetration. General Bradley took over control of
the group of armies on the south flank. He ordered

up the 101st Airborne Division, which had been in reserve, to hold Bastogne, road center for all the middle Ardennes, while the Seventh Army slid leftward to take over the front of the Third. Patton brought that force up to attack the south flank of the bulge at a speed rarely seen in war; his 5th Division moved 69 miles in a day and was in action by nightfall.

The key of the battle proved to be Bastogne. The 101st had barely arrived before it was surrounded, and though joined by retreating elements of the 10th Armored Division, it was so thoroughly cut off that it had to be supplied by air for a week. During that week it was attacked all around the perimeter of its position day and night. The defense was heroic to the last degree. When the Germans sent in a flag of truce requesting surrender, and accompanied it with maps to show that the position of the defenders was hopeless, they were met with the simple reply "Nuts!" from Brigadier-General A. C. McAuliffe. The phrase is likely to endure long in American memory.

Lacking the roads thus denied them, the Germans had to swing a circuit northward, and being stopped by the British in their progress toward Liège had to make another swing southward in the direction of our supply depots. On the 22nd the weather cleared; the whole of our tactical air forces were thrown onto their supply columns and

armored forces moving through the narrow channels of the mountains, and as these convoys were
numerous, the destruction was great. By the 25th
Patton's armored formations were making their
presence so much felt that Rundstedt had to detail
many of his troops for defensive duties. All the fire
went out of his drive and on the next day besieged
Bastogne was relieved.

Now the problem for the enemy became one of
getting his men out of the most forward areas of advance while under constant attack and with all the
roads leading from the area heavily shelled. He
retreated in good order and so slowly that it was
the end of January before he was back across the
frontier. But the problem was never really solved,
for in the course of the battle he lost 110,000 prisoners and another 110,000 casualties of other types,
along with the full mechanical equipment of two
armored armies.

This was the end of the German strategic reserve.
When the Russians launched a prodigious attack all
along the eastern front on January 22, there were
no reinforcements to send against them. The whole
front began rolling back; and though the Nazis had
anticipated the attack, they were by no means prepared for the facts that it was made in greater force
than any other offensive of the war and was backed
by transportation equipment that made demolitions of no effect. A month from the beginning of

the movement it was on the Oder, threatening Stettin, Dresden, and even Berlin. General Eisenhower could prepare his own spring offensive in the full confidence that if he achieved a break-through anywhere, he would go all the way.

On the Lorraine front the Germans had launched covering attacks in support of their Ardennes drive of December, 1944, but the men of the Seventh Army merely pulled out of the advanced positions that had been held by the Third and retired to the old fortifications of the Maginot Line. On these the Germans failed to make any impression. Still farther south, the French in Alsace had worked through the Belfort Gap into the plain during the fall. As winter came on, they operated an encirclement with the help of the Seventh Army units coming down from the north, cut off a number of German formations, and by the end of January had cleared the whole left bank of the Rhine. General Eisenhower held this long stretch with relatively light forces, concentrating toward his strategic left, while General Patton's Third Army gradually worked down to take over part of the positions it had previously held along the borders of the Palatinate.

These preliminary moves, with preparations behind the lines, occupied most of February, 1945. On the 9th of that month the Canadians on the

north started another flank-clearing operation in
the region where the Rhine makes its westward
bend. Each army down the line was to swing into
the attack in succession, with Simpson's American
Ninth making the main effort, straight across the
Roer toward Düsseldorf. Floods delayed the
Ninth's movement, the Germans concentrated
against the Canadians and stopped them after some
initial gains. It was Rundstedt's last success and
used his last reserves. When the Ninth did attack
on the moonlit night of February 23 under cover
of chemical smokes, it broke right through with
surprising ease. Half a dozen bridgeheads were
established before dawn, before noon bridges were
up and armor was crossing them, striking into the
rear areas of the troops opposing the Canadians
and for the Rhine bridges across which these troops
were supported.

Swarms of Allied planes covered the advance.
The Germans could make no head against them,
their communications began to go, and on the night
of March 1 their High Command ordered with-
drawal from this whole northern salient down to
the mountains that enclose the Meuse. The retreating forces blew all the Rhine bridges as they
retired and fought well during the movement; but
there was no time for the elaborate mining and
demolitions which had covered similar retreats in
Africa and Italy, and great numbers of the enemy

were cut off and captured by our armor in the open plains.

Still more prisoners were taken when the Ninth began to fan southward toward Cologne while Hodges' First attacked on its part of the front. All the stone villages had been converted into fortresses, but the Nazis were now badly outnumbered and the mobility of our forces was such as to increase the effect of their numbers. When a knot of resistance was encountered, planes, tanks, and self-propelled guns appeared within the hour to lay down an unbearable concentration of fire. Cologne, a ruined city, fell on March 7.

At Bonn the enemy tried to hold, in order to let some of their troops from the southern part of the front reach the Rhine, but on that same March 7 the 9th Armored Division broke through loose German lines to reach the river at Remagen south of Bonn. One of the great' bridges stands there. The 9th found it damaged by Allied aerial bombs and mined for demolition, but still standing, and defended by only a handful of infantry who were driven off before they could blow the bridge. The 9th crossed at once, and on the opposite bank began to spread out and dig in. They were counterattacked that day only by weak infantry formations. During the night the German area commander got some artillery together and next morning attacked again, energetically shelling both the bridge itself

and the American position, from a chain of hills east of the river. But by this time the bridgehead was increasing rapidly both in strength and extent, for General Hodges had at once recognized the importance of this foothold beyond a stream which is one of the toughest military obstacles of the world, and had called off every other operation to pour reinforcements in behind the 9th Armored.

As both sides brought up troops a major battle developed, the Allied planes maintaining a continuous patrol over the bridge and German planes constantly trying to break through to bomb. An attack on March 11 captured most of the German observation posts in the dominating hills but could not be driven much deeper. On the other hand our forces made steady progress in extending the bridgehead along the flanks, where our artillery fire could take their positions in enfilade from the west bank. On the 17th the bridge collapsed, but by that date there were already three pontoon bridges in support and two more were shortly added, over which the whole First Army poured into an area that was now fifteen miles long by eight miles deep.

But by this date the truly fatal blow had been struck. From the Rhine at a point just south of Remagen runs the jagged range of the Eiffel Mountains, cut by few and easily defensible passes to the north. This chain formed the northern defense of the Palatinate, which on its west and south was

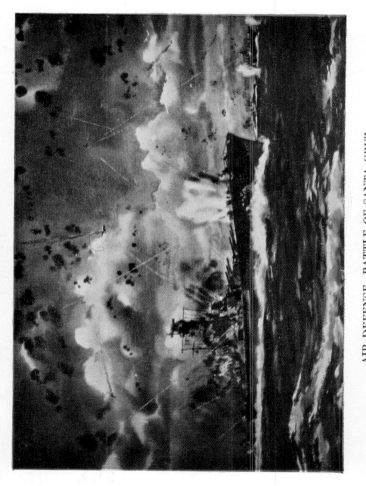

AIR DEFENSE: BATTLE OF SANTA CRUZ

From the water color by Dwight C. Shepler, Commander U.S.N.R.

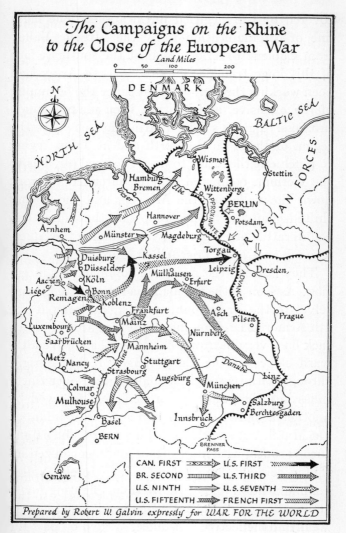

The Campaigns on the Rhine
to the Close of the European War

Land Miles

Prepared by Robert W. Galvin expressly for WAR FOR THE WORLD

covered by the Siegfried fortifications. The main line of communication is by the Moselle Valley from Coblenz to Trier. Against the southern face of this huge triangle, Patch's Seventh Army had been working through obstacles since the beginning of the offensive, and had not been making much progress. Patton's Third Army attacked in the region of Prüm on the north and at Trier, trying to pinch out the latter town. It seemed obvious to the German command that he intended to work down the valley of the Moselle, and the enemy shifted many of their troops in that direction, counterattacking vigorously and holding the American advance after Trier fell on March 2.

They misread the American commander's intention. As soon as the Germans had committed themselves to the Trier counterattack, Patton put the 4th Armored Division into the Prüm area in an attack on a very narrow front along the steep southward slopes of the Eiffel range. It broke right through with scarcely a casualty, going over thirty miles in a day, and was immediately followed by another armored division and several of infantry. On March 7 it struck the Rhine near Coblenz and turned south, with more armor and mechanized infantry coming along behind. The Moselle Valley communication line of the Germans fighting far to the west was cut; Patton's spearhead, meeting only weak and ineffective resistance, pressed on past the

mouth of that stream, which was crossed on March
14. Three days later both Worms and Mainz were
taken and the 4th Armored rushed on up the bank
of the Rhine to cut the communications of the
whole group of armies in the Palatinate.

These had begun to retreat when Coblenz fell, for
the German command had so concentrated on holding its fortified frontiers that there was nothing
within the rear areas to halt Patton's rush. The retreating troops were now vigorously attacked both
by the Third Army along the Moselle Valley and
from the south by the Seventh, which in the intervening weeks had worked through most of the vast
minefields. General Patch of the Seventh threw his
armor into the pursuit, and now the fast, long-
range American tanks were as far superior to German armor as the latter had been superior in close
fighting. The Nazi formations could only escape by
leaving larger and larger proportions of their numbers as self-sacrificing rear guards, and, even so,
not 10 percent of the men in all that group of
armies got away across the Rhine.

At Allied Headquarters the passage of the Rhine
had loomed as an operation quite equal in difficulty
to the landing in Normandy. Elaborate preparations for it had been made, especially in the north,
where Marshal Montgomery, with the British and
Canadian forces and the American Ninth Army,

was facing the great industrial district of the Ruhr,
where the bulk of the defenders had been concentrated. On the evening of March 23, 1945, the
crossing was simultaneously begun by the Second
British and American Ninth armies, two airborne
divisions being dropped ahead of the line of attack.
The effort was everywhere successful and the two
armies advanced abreast against opposition that
was often tenacious but could find little good
ground for defense in an area where Allied mecha-
nization, ably seconded from the air, gave our forces
such extreme mobility.

In the meantime the Third Army elements had
seized two more crossings at Mainz and Oppen-
heim, and on March 22 Patton began sending his
formations across, driving straight east against opposition everywhere weak. The armies that should
have defended this area had been destroyed in the
Palatinate, and though Hitler called every German
to arms in defense of the fatherland and found
weapons for a good many, he could not provide
them with military organization or training. How
far the disintegration of the once-great Nazi armies
had progressed was made clear when Hodges of the
First Army delivered a general attack from the
Remagen bridgehead. At the north end of the
bridgehead area a small river, the Sieg, flows into
the Rhine from the east at right angles between
steep hills. During the previous two weeks Hodges'

men had made several probing attacks against this river line and the Germans shifted a portion of their Ruhr forces southward to hold it. On March 25 the First attacked in force, but to the surprise of the enemy, in a southeasterly direction, right away from the Sieg line. They broke through easily, flung one column off southward to capture Frankfurt, then drove straight east and north in a wide sweep outside the whole Ruhr area, the general direction being Kassel-Paderborn.

The Third Army joined in this great wheel, parallel with but outside the orbit of the First. The Seventh, which had by now forced its own crossings, drove east and southeast to cut the roads to the Bavarian highlands, where it was thought that the fanatic remnants of the Nazis might attempt to stand. Wherever these had leaders and supplies they did fight on, notably in the Ruhr, which had to be reduced piece by piece through the attacks of the First and the Ninth, and the new Fifteenth Army. But throughout April the operation of cutting Germany up into parts went on virtually unchecked, while the Russians were winning Berlin, house by house. On the 9th of that month the Allied forces in Italy made a general assault on the positions that had held there so long, and this attack too swept everything before it. The whole German structure was now in a state of collapse; resistance in most cases became merely formal, and after

Hitler committed suicide in the blazing ruins of Berlin an emergency government gave its unconditional surrender to the Allies on May 7, 1945.

To its own people this government explained that their country had been overborne by an accumulation of mechanical weapons. This was untrue. The Germans had been beaten because on the sea they could find no means of preventing our troops from reaching Europe; because in the air they could find none of keeping our bombers from pounding their transportation system to pieces and cutting off their sources of fuel; and, above all, because on land they could find no officers who used the means at hand as well as ours, whatever those means might be.

CHAPTER XVIII

THE END OF JAPAN

THE first B-29 raid from Saipan against Japan was flown on November 24, 1944, and was rapidly followed by others. The results were somewhat disappointing. The quality of information from within the beleaguered country was not all that could be desired, but it was clear from photo-reconnaissance that, in comparison to the effort and materials expended, the damage was comparatively slight. In the meantime, as soon as the organizational period of the new base was complete, the Army Air Force had sent one of its best young operational officers, Major-General Curtis LeMay, to take charge. He reached the conclusion that even with the accurate bombsight it was difficult to obtain sufficient hits on targets that were usually small and always well distributed. As a result he sent the big bombers in at levels under 10,000 feet in a trial raid late in December. This time the results were thoroughly satisfactory; nor were the losses at the lower level of bombing such as to discourage the operation.

But as time and the bombing program went on,

two flaws appeared. The first was that at these lower levels the big planes suffered damage from both anti-aircraft fire and the attentions of Japanese fighters. The damage was not sufficient to bring many of them down at once, but a number of the expensive machines were lost in forced landings at sea. Submarines of the American fleet worked out an admirable rescue service, picking up more than 500 men. But still the loss in planes was serious. The second difficulty lay in the Japanese reaction to the bombing program. They sent down medium bombers of their own from the Bonins to make suicidal crash landings among the planes parked on the Marianas fields, and though many of these bombers were shot down before reaching their destination, enough attained it to make the counterattack a matter of concern. Nor did repeated air strikes on the Bonins fields appreciably reduce this activity.

The navy's own strategic program was still for the capture of some of the Ryukyus, but for the moment the support of the B-29 program became more important. As soon as General MacArthur's Luzon operation had been placed on a self-sustaining basis, therefore, the fleet hurried north to carry through preparations which had already been made for attacking Iwo Jima in the Volcano Islands, the southern extension of the Bonin group. Iwo Jima lies 750 miles from Tokyo. Long-range fighters

from it could cover the B-29s on their flights, and other fighters could eliminate enemy counterattacks at their inception; moreover, it would afford a way station for crippled planes.

The ships were now once more under the command of Admiral Spruance, with Admiral Mitscher in charge of the carriers. The troops for the operation were three divisions of Marines (3rd, 4th, and 5th) commanded by Major-General Harry Schmidt, who had led the ground forces on Saipan. The island has a deep coating of sifting ash. A tall volcano rises at its southern end and at the northern end a long slope leads up to a high plateau from which another volcano rises. There were only two practicable beaches, both so well commanded by the elevated positions that a surprise landing would be impossible. Therefore, the attack had to be a straight frontal one, at a place where the enemy expected it, and nothing would serve but overwhelming force applied with the greatest energy.

This application began on February 16, 1945, a year to the day from the first attack on Truk. The fast carriers ran close up to Japan for a strike at Tokyo and the plane factories and airfields around it. There was heavy aerial fighting; we lost 49 planes and the enemy 322, besides numbers destroyed on the ground. Meanwhile the battleships had moved in against Iwo, which they subjected

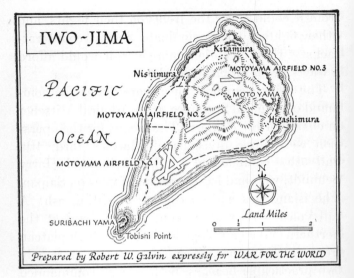

IWO-JIMA

Kitamura

Nishimura   MOTOYAMA AIRFIELD NO.3

PACIFIC   MOTO YAMA

MOTOYAMA AIRFIELD NO. 2   Higashimura

OCEAN

MOTOYAMA AIRFIELD NO.1

N

Land Miles

SURIBACHI YAMA

Tobishi Point   0   ½   1   2

Prepared by Robert W. Galvin expressly for WAR FOR THE WORLD

to a shelling more intense than those at Kwajalein
or Peleliu, combing over every inch of it for days.
Escort carriers added a bomb attack; so did army
planes working from Saipan, and the fast carrier
force on its return from the Tokyo strike. At dawn
on February 19, landings began, with the 4th and
5th Marine Divisions going in.

They met some mortar fire as they approached
the beach and a couple of LSTs were hit, but this
first stage was crossed with comparative ease. But
as the Marines attempted to advance from their
beach the true strength and nature of the defenses
became manifest. The beach itself was almost
knee-deep in the gritty volcanic ash which clogged

the tracks of tanks and offered no concealment whatever. Under this ash the whole island was honeycombed with an elaborate system of caves, tunnels, and pillboxes, so deep they had hardly been touched at all by that furious preliminary bombardment. From every one of these the Japanese opened fire with weapons of all descriptions; from the plateau on the north, from Mt. Suribachi on the south, came the shells of big guns and a new, very formidable type of rocket.

Once more it was touch and go, with some possibility that the landing could not be made good. Supplies could not be landed nor the wounded evacuated; there was no artillery ashore. The Marines clung doggedly to their ground, working forward to knock out pillbox after pillbox at close range. They had one advantage seldom found in previous landings, in that the island was small with deep water close inshore. Destroyers of the fleet moved in and, aided by new fire-control methods, laid shells with pinpoint accuracy as little as twenty yards ahead of the advancing troops. They were seldom able to smash the heavily concreted pillboxes, but their fire kept the defenders under cover while the Marines crept forward with demolition charges—normally losing several of their number by fire from flanking pillboxes in the process.

In this manner the attackers fought their way across the narrow neck of the island, on the first

night. During that night the Japanese came out of their holes in a heavy counterattack, which was beaten off under the constant glare of star shells, and in the morning the slow advance began again. It was February 23 before Mt. Suribachi had been stormed and some relief obtained from the plunging mortar fire that had caused so many casualties. Amphibian tanks got ashore after this; two days later the attackers were fighting in the main village toward the north end of the island and clearing out a system of more than 100 interconnected caves, each 30 to 40 feet deep. It was well into March before the last fighting was done. When it was over, 20,000 Japanese were dead and the Marines had had the bloodiest battle of their history, with 20,196 casualties of their own. Offshore the fleet was under constant attack from Kamikaze which sank one escort carrier and inflicted terrific injuries on two of the large carriers.

But even before the island was entirely won, bulldozers were at work improving the airfields for the use of our fighters, and on March 9 the great fleet of B-29s with full fighter escort struck Tokyo. They carried nothing but fire bombs, which they spread broadcast across a section of the city where small airplane parts were manufactured in the homes. A wind fanned the flames; all measures of protection proved futile and over a third of the Japanese capital burned to the ground.

The way was now clear for the attack on the Ryukyus. It was directed at Okinawa, the largest of the group, only 370 miles from Kyushu, 65 miles long and irregular in shape, with a rugged and wooded northern portion, the southern half well populated, but much cut up by ravines. Preliminary estimates were that some 80,000 Japanese troops held the place. To overcome them the new Tenth Army was detailed under Lieutenant-General S. B. Buckner; it consisted of a corps of Marines and one composed of three divisions of army troops (27th, 77th, and 96th) that had frequently worked with the Navy. The whole fleet was in support, together with a powerful squadron of British ships.

Offshore from the southern tip of Okinawa are some small islands, the Kerama Retto. These afford a fairly well-sheltered anchorage against the typhoons that are very frequent in that part of the world. They were attacked on March 26, 1945, while mine sweepers of the fleet were working off Okinawa itself. By March 31 they were in our hands, and a vast fleet of supply ships and repair vessels moved in, in preparation for the landing on Okinawa's western shore the next morning. The landing was accomplished readily and with little loss, the army getting 50,000 men ashore by evening of the first day and holding a beachhead two miles in depth. The drive was across the island's

narrow waist; by April 4 the opposite shore had been reached, and the Marines turned north against the wooded ground, where the Japanese were expected to be found in force among the hills, while the army men swung south against the populated section and its formal defenses.

But by April 4, also, the campaign had developed a feature new to the Pacific war. Japanese planes, generally in small groups, had attacked our mine sweepers and their covering vessels off Okinawa. This was anticipated; the novelty lay in the fact that nearly all these attacks were by Kamikaze, the suicide planes, which succeeded in sinking a couple of the mine sweepers. Among the Kerama Retto Islands were found a number of small fast boats heavily charged with explosives, obviously designed to be used as suicide craft. It began to look as though the Japanese boasts of converting their entire air force into a Kamikaze corps were not far short of the fact.

These fanatics had been gathering on the Kyushu airfields and it was of the utmost importance to keep them from getting in among the transports and supply vessels off Okinawa. Admiral Spruance took the fleet north for a series of carrier strikes, while Admiral Frazer ran south with the British fleet for a similar attack on the Shikishima islands.

The dual move provoked a remarkable battle. The Japanese had planned a massive Kamikaze

strike against our fleet while their own shoul\
run down the East China Sea to attack the Okinawa beachhead. The American carrier strike came
on them a little too soon for their plan. Several
hundred planes were destroyed on the Kyushu airfields and the fleet that was to attack our Okinawa
beachhead was reduced to the new battleship
Yamato, a light cruiser, and ten destroyers, which
nevertheless began the run down the East China
Sea.

It was spotted, and on April 7 Admiral Mitscher
flew off the fleet's planes in a massive strike. All
day they hammered at the enemy ships; *Yamato*,
the cruiser and four of the destroyers went down,
and three more of the destroyers were crippled.
But at the same time the enemy attacked our fleet
with a swarm of nearly 600 Kamikaze. Several of
our light craft were damaged or sunk and one big
carrier badly mauled. Four days later, with the
fleet still off Kyushu, came another wave of Kamikaze and again there was damage.

On April 12 the Japs shifted their attack to the
transports off Okinawa beachhead, bringing in a
new type of suicide plane in addition to the others
—the Baka, a rocket-propelled, and manned, aerial
torpedo, which was carried by a larger plane and
released near its destination. Our patrol shot down
151 Japanese that day; and on our return to Kyushu on April 15–16, in another air battle of the

ᴊame type, 249 more were destroyed. But on both occasions some of our ships were hit and the impact of the bomb-loaded planes always resulted in frightful damage and heavy casualties.

THE situation caused concern, for although few ships were sunk, and those all among the lighter types, many of the big carriers had to go in for repairs. The strength of the fleet was being steadily cut down, while the ground battle on Okinawa seemed endless. The light resistance our forces had encountered after landing on April 1, 1945, proved to be only the first phase of a new type of defense.

At the north end of the island the Marines encountered only moderate opposition and by the middle of April had cleared the rough ground there except for mopping-up operations. In the south, after a rapid early advance, the army troops ran into a system of fortifications that verged on the fantastic. The ground was cut up by ravines sheltering some natural limestone caves; these had been added to and built up with tunnels until the whole island was almost as much of a network as the much smaller Iwo Jima. This setup was familiar, but the Japanese had added the new feature of quantities of artillery, including mortars of a new type and of gigantic size, which permitted the defenders of the caves to take far more aggressive action than had been encountered elsewhere.

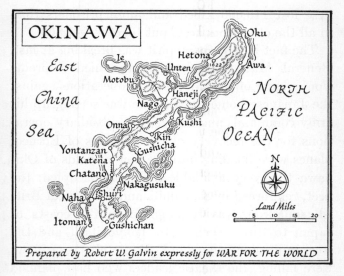

OKINAWA

East China Sea

Oku
Hetona
Ie
Unten
1622
Awa
Motobu
Haneji
Nago
Kushi
Onna
Kin
Gushicha
Yontanzan
Katena
Chatano
Nakagusuku
Naha
Shuri
Itoman
Gushichan

NORTH PACIFIC OCEAN

N

Land Miles
0 5 10 15 20

Prepared by Robert W. Galvin expressly for WAR FOR THE WORLD

The number of their troops also proved to be a considerable underestimate, and they did not hesitate to use these troops in almost continual suicidal night counterattacks, one of which nearly drove the 27th Division into the sea. The whole campaign evolved into an exhausting form of siege warfare, in which each individual Japanese position had to be taken by hand as on Iwo Jima. The divisions were rotated in action, and the Marine Corps was brought down from the north to help out the army. Inch by inch progress was made until June 21, when organized resistance ended. The island had cost us 39,000 casualties ashore, plus another 10,000 in the fleet offshore. The Japa-

nese lost 110,000 killed and more prisoners than in all the other conquests put together—7,800.

The fact is that their spirit was breaking at last. General MacArthur had been named Supreme Commander of ground forces for operations against the Japanese home islands. He was setting up his army commands and conducting subsidiary operations for the recovery of the oil ports of Borneo; planes were flooding into the new airfields of Okinawa till every available inch was occupied; the fleet, reinforced by new units and a powerful British squadron, was running up to the coasts of Japan to throw shells into Tokyo itself and the steel mills along the shore. While all these blows were falling, the fanatic leaders who had planned the conquest of half a world were making a series of discoveries. The Okinawa campaign had caused concern in the American command, but it had really been the last gasp of the Japanese air force; they lost over 3,400 planes and their replacement capacity was now so seriously impaired that the Japanese High Command was forced to order the remaining machines withheld for defense against the invasion of Japan. Even for the remaining planes, there was a serious shortage of gasoline, and the capture of Okinawa had placed our ships and planes in position from which they cut off any further supply of the natural product.

Many of the best formations of the Japanese

army had been destroyed among the islands were now cut off in the south. In fact, the spring of 1945 saw a general movement of Japanese troops from the newly won lands in southern China up toward Manchuria and the coasts of the Sea of Japan. That area was the home of the army that had started the nation on its career of aggression. There it expected to make a stand even after the loss of the home islands, with some idea of wearing out our patience. This hope vanished on August 8 when the Soviet Government declared war and sent its powerful, battle-experienced forces through the passes into Manchuria. But two days before that, on August 6, there had already occurred an event which threw the Russian attack into the shade.

A B-29 of the strategic air force passed over the city of Hiroshima and dropped a single bomb in which the energy of the atom was released. Since the beginning of the war, British, Canadian, and American scientists had been working on the problem of harnessing that energy. So had the Germans, and the fear that they might attain the goal first had been one of the reasons for General Eisenhower's hurry in the early spring of 1945. Now it had been found, and the results were all that imagination predicted. Hiroshima, previously undamaged, was completely destroyed and something like 80,000 people were killed. Three days later another

The Position Versus Japan

U. S. S. R.

KARAFUTO

KURILE IS.

MANCHURIA

Amur

Outer Mongolia

Inner Mongolia

Sea of Japan

KOREA

Tokyo

JAPAN

Yellow Sea

Yellow

Yangtze

CHINA

Chungking

Shanghai

PACIFIC OCEAN

RYUKYU RETTO

FORMOSA

N

Hong Kong

BURMA

FRENCH

SIAM

INDO-CHINA

SOUTH CHINA SEA

Manila

PHILIPPINES

MALAY PENINSULA

NETHERLANDS INDIES

Singapore

Territory Surrendered by Japan—14 August, 1945

Prepared by Robert W. Galvin expressly for WAR FOR THE WORLD

atomic bomb similarly pulverized most of the great port city of Nagasaki and on August 14, 1945, the Japanese government capitulated.

As the Germans had done, the Japanese explained their surrender on the basis of the mechanical odds—the atomic bomb. But we have ample evidence that even before the first bomb was dropped the leaders of the empire had already decided that it was useless to continue a struggle in which all operations were reduced to a suicidal passive defense. This had been accomplished by the ability of our now unchallengeable navy to transmit to any point overwhelming forces of soldiers who, through their mobility and command of the air, were always superior to the enemy in ground operations.

By their own reports after the war, neither the Japanese nor the German enemy was particularly impressed by the performance of these soldiers as infantry. Our men lacked the fanaticism of the former and the exquisite skill which the latter had acquired through years of devotion to no other business but that of war. Yet the casualties of the American infantry service were high—perhaps exceptionally high—being nearly half of the 1,200,-000 casualties our armed forces suffered during the conflict. Out of a total of eleven million men borne on the rolls in army and navy together, this indicates sufficient courage and devotion for the pur-

pose. The fact is that neither the Germans (though they had spent years in working out the science of war) nor the Japanese (who had begun consciously to prepare for the conflict as early as 1927) realized the implications for modern war that modern technology and modern methods possessed: the fact that the infantry soldier was no longer the arbiter of the battlefield nor the brave and capable seaman of the naval action.

The Germans, who affected so little concern about our infantry, were indignant about American artillery and planes, which struck them down without an opportunity for reply. They protested bitterly that the fight was never "fair"; that in every action our superior transportation equipment gave us the advantage of numbers. The Japanese naval commander in the notable instance of the Battle of Empress Augusta Bay (November 1, 1943) withdrew from the action because he was being repeatedly hit by enemies he could not even see (his own radar did not work) and of whose force he could form no estimate. Over both Germans and Japanese the victory for our side was technological.

This does not in the least detract from the courage of the men who handled the weapons. World War II was so vast that individual acts of heroism became insignificant, yet no war in which Americans had been engaged produced more of them,

not in absolute terms alone, but in proportion to
the numbers engaged. No war produced so few
instances of panic or cowardice, whether in relative
or absolute numbers. This fact is perhaps related
to the other fact that for the first time since 1861
our dearest ideals and ideas were engaged. Nor
does the technological side of the triumph detract
from the intelligence of our leaders. Rather it in-
creases the respect one must feel for them, as the
leaders of the American Revolution are respected
because they used correctly the American riflemen
fighting from under cover.

But it is important for us to recognize that the
victory was technological, not on the battlefield
alone. This technology brought something new to
the whole science and art of war, and indeed to
that of human collaboration for the achievement
of a great purpose; it was the specific American
contribution to the general victory. The British
made an immense contribution to that victory; for
a whole year they held back the European Axis,
armed with the strength and industry of a continent, and they had resiliency enough at the close
of that ordeal to win one of the few absolutely decisive victories of the whole conflict. The Russians
contributed enormously; it was they who contained, dispersed, and finally broke the backs of
those German armies who had run unchecked from
the Vistula to the Pyrenees and the Nile. They

paid for it with seven million casualties as against
our million.

Yet both of these contributions, quantitatively
huge, were made within the old frames of reference,
within the bounds of the old art of war, in which
strategy, tactics, and courage are the determining
factors.

What America introduced was a new art of war
in which logistics usurped many of the functions
of the other branches—the thing the Nazis referred
to as "total war" but never quite understood or
found the means to put into practice. This may
be demonstrated statistically. It is an old truism
of naval war that, unless a conflict becomes very
lengthy indeed, the number of ships with which a
combatant begins the war are in the main those
with which he ends it, very small craft excepted.
In World War II this remained true for the British
navy, the German, the Japanese, and the Italian.
The American navy began the war with a force
of something over 300 combatant ships. At the
close it possessed 1,167 major warships and only a
single vessel of the pre-war fleet was still of sufficient first-line efficiency to participate in the final
attacks on Japan. A program for building over
80,000 landing craft had been undertaken and
nearly 60,000 of them had been built. All the com-
batants made some use of women in uniform for
various rear area services; the American Wacs,

Waves, and Spars outnumbered all the rest of the women's services put together.

In this new art of war it was unimportant that we brought to the field only 100 combat divisions against 125 Japanese and nearly 100 German (the remainder of their divisions were pinned down and largely destroyed by the Russians). The important factor was that with the aid of the British, on land and sea, the Allied forces possessed a continual superiority of fire power at every important point of contact. It was in this domain of coöperation all the way back to the factories that the American contribution lay. The Germans and Japanese regarded infantry fighting as the index and critical factor in war; the American contribution was to make it one element in a vast complex, here for the first time successfully integrated.

BIBLIOGRAPHICAL NOTE

FOR a variety of reasons the naval side of World War II has been much more adequately documented than operations on land. Probably the best brief general history is Shugg and De Weerd's *World War II, A Concise History;* but it suffers from some inaccuracies in the treatment of the naval war and from the authors' anxiety to mention everything, so that a sense of proportion is lost. An excellent running account of the war will be found in the current files of the *Field Artillery Journal,* though this also is affected by the myopia inevitably attendant upon the writing about events which are still in progress.

The official reports of the leaders in the war, compiled soon after it was over, are of the greatest value, and those of General Marshall and Marshal Montgomery are written with a skill which would make them interesting reading matter regardless of subject. General Marshall's report is titled *The Winning of the War in Europe and the Pacific;* Marshal Montgomery's, *Operations in North-West Europe. The Report of the U. S. Army Air Forces* by General H. H. Arnold, the *Reports to the Secretary of the Navy* by Admiral Ernest J. King, and *Eisenhower's Own Story of the War* belong in the same category. Much material on American as well as British aviation forces is contained in *Bomber Offensive* by Marshal of the R. A. F. Sir Arthur Harris.

In some details, particularly with reference to the strategic concepts, it is difficult to reconcile Marshal Montgomery's account with those of Eisenhower and Marshall. The reader will find Captain Harry C. Butcher's *My Three Years with Eisenhower* useful. Lt. Col. A. H. Burne's *Strategy as Exemplified in the Second World War* offers illuminating comment. Ralph Ingersoll's *Top Secret* is violent, controversial, and often demonstrably inaccurate, but it contains some useful detail on the European campaigns. A useful corrective is supplied by Major-General Sir Francis de Guingand's *Operation Victory*. The U. S. Army Historical Section has published and is continuing to publish a long series of studies on individual operations. They are somewhat uneven in character but the best are very good indeed; those on *Omaha Beachhead*, *St. Lô*, and the *Volturno* deserve special mention.

Two quasi-official publications head the list on the naval war. As this is written only two volumes of Professor S. E. Morison's *History of U. S. Naval Operations in World War II* have appeared; the list is to be extended to fourteen. Captain Walter Karig, with various collaborators, has produced three volumes of his *Battle Report*. This work presents a more humanized picture of events, but the first two volumes, dealing with the operations from Pearl Harbor to Coral Sea and the war in the Atlantic, were written while the conflict was still in progress and under the strictest censorship rules. Accordingly they are frequently lacking in completeness.

An understanding of the naval war is almost impossible without reference to Bernard Brodie's *Guide to*